Sanctified Street

Just Another Story

EDWARD
ROY

SANCTIFIED STREET: *Just Another Story*

Copyright © 2025 Edward Roy

ISBN (Paperback): 979-8-89672-021-8
ISBN (Ebook): 979-8-89672-022-5

Printed in the United States of America.

PROMINENT
BOOKS

5830 E 2nd St, Ste 7000 #9983
Casper, WY 82609
USA

CONTENTS

A WORD FROM REVEREND ROY

SURE, IT SOUNDS like I'm trying to sell you a used car with no engine but that is so far from my purpose. God's purpose for me is to…. Once you understand your purpose God will help you harness your inner strength. I will share if you are involved in the game and have a parole officer, or I am speaking with you in a prison setting, or you are reading one of my articles in a prison setting; ask yourself have you really mastered the street life game? I am asking because if you have, you wouldn't be reading this in a jail cell. Or listening to me speak at a prison speaking event. Reading this in a jail cell means you got caught. I got caught many times. As good as I may have been at the game, I was not good enough not to get caught more than once. Getting caught could be the best thing to ever happen to you. It should certainly make you consider as I did, a new line of work. A new way of life. Are you mad after reading that sentence? If you're not you should be. God's plan for you was never this life. God's children are built to succeed. I'm not telling you what I heard, I'm telling you what I know.

Finally, know that you can call on God anywhere, anytime. Life is a participation sport; step up, own your shenanigans (sins), repent (ask for forgiveness), and move into your purpose. Speak to the resource person at your facility for access to resources to help you move forward in a positive manner.

ONCE UPON A CRIMINAL

I WAS BORN in Minneapolis, Minnesota and lived with my grand-mother and Great-grandmother till I was about 6 months old. Then my 14-year-old mother along with a guy I did not know moved to Wexford St in Detroit Michigan on the west side of Wayne County and 8 mile (8 mile is what could be described as a frontage road). In Detroit it was important to know where you were at all times because if you ended up in a neighborhood where you were not known, had no affiliation, or were lost it often did not turn out well for you.

We lived in a flat like apartment with several other families. A flat is a self-contained housing unit that occupies only part of a building. An example would be an apartment above a store. In this flat I remember us sharing a kitchen with other families because the flats had one or two bedrooms connected to a living room. Some of the flats had a bathroom. But you would have to go through a bedroom in your flat to get to the bathroom. Some flats included a kitchen but no bathroom.

Which is why the building, had a kitchen and a bathroom for everyone in the building to use. My family and I felt blessed because we did not have to go out in the cold hallway to use the bathroom and bathe ourselves. My aunt did not have a bathroom in her flat. But that was probably best with the girls and johns running in and out of the building all the time.

1

There were always lots of children and lots of women, but few men living in these flats. The women and children treated one another as family. With the children calling the women auntie. And the children in the building calling each other cousin. Although, there were lots of men coming and going through the flat they were not part of the family unit those who lived in the flat had created for themselves.

The flat that I lived in had a lot of women bringing guys in and out of the place, I would see these men handing the women lots of money. The men coming and going were johns (men who purchased sexual services from women). At the time I did not know why these men were coming and going. I did not know they were called johns. I just knew there was a lot of them. They would stay for an hour or so and then leave.

The building I stayed in also had two very, big black men standing at the front door and the back door. I knew they were there in case one of the johns started acting up. But if the johns got beat up or robbed and they asked these huge black men who secured the front and back door, "Did you see that?" These very, big black men would look at the john, shake their head and say, "I didn't see nothin." The john would ask repeatedly, "Man you didn't see that? You didn't see what just happened?" And the black men would answer, "No" or "I didn't see nothin'." every time.

While living in Detroit I picked up some bad habits outside of joining a gang. In Detroit it was not unusual for a child or anyone else to see a dead person laying on the sidewalk as older kids went through the dead person's pockets. So bad habits were not just easy to pick up, they were demonstrated by the people around me.

The guy who my mom and I moved to Detroit with, now was my stepdad, drove Greyhound bus. I don't know this for sure, but I do think he was much older than, my mom. I did take on my stepdad's last name and his family treated me as one of their own. My stepdad had nine brothers and two sisters. One of my stepdad's sisters was Aunt Charlene who would take care of me while my mom went to school.

I called my stepdad, dad even though he would beat me with his fist, or the cord attached to the iron. I hated him and I felt he hated me because I was not his real son. But all and all he was the only dad I knew. He provided for me, my mom, and my other siblings. My step-dad belonged to a real big family in Detroit, so that helped me be safe on the streets. I loved my stepdad's family and all of the uncles, aunts and cousins that accepted me as part of their family.

My Aunt Charlene who I mentioned would keep me while my mom was at school; would tell me, "Lee, even though you are a young man, always remember to respect the game. Like it or not. If you don't stay in front of the money, the money won't stay behind you." My aunt shared this with me at the tender age of eleven.

Even though it may seem inappropriate to some. She was sharing what she had. She was sharing what she knew. Even though I was only eleven when I heard this advice about staying in front of my money, I believed my aunt was telling me not to let anyone take my money. I saw how my aunt and her girls were using these men, these johns. I knew at a very, early age what side of the game I wanted to be on. I wanted to be on the side that took the money (again), not the side that gave the money (a loss).

In the summer of 1964, I moved back to Minneapolis, MN where I was born. North Minneapolis with my grandmother to be exact. Even though I lived in North Minneapolis I had friends and relatives in north and south Minneapolis. Minneapolis even today is a very cliquish city. People pretty much stayed on the side of town they lived in. And hung out in their own territory. It's crazy because North Minneapolis is about a 10-minute car ride from South Minneapolis. And Saint Paul is about a 20-minute car ride from Minneapolis. But I didn't care about how cliquish the city was I had friends on both sides of town.

Living with grandmother was fun. Her and my great grandmother spoiled me. I asked my grandmother for a typewriter so my friend and I could create short stories and comic books. My friend would create the drawings and I would write the stories. There was a store located in downtown Minneapolis called Woolworth's when I was a child. There was a brand-new typewriter in the window of Woolworth's. I told my grandmother I wanted that typewriter and she bought it for me. I know she bought it to encourage me to write.

The teacher at Lincoln Elementary located in North Minneapolis who made me feel like I was somebody, was a white teacher named Miss Larson. I was in the sixth grade and Miss Larson would use my comic books to encourage me to read. It was this encouragement that allowed me to create the comic books with my friend. My inspiration was Superman and the Green Hornet. The Green Hornet had an emerald green Cadillac and a partner named Cato.

Cato was an Asian man that knew karate. The actor who played Cato was a real-ife Karate' expert named Bruce Lee. All my friends and I loved Bruce Lee karate' movies. When the Green Hornet would get into fights with criminals, the best fights would be when Cato would join the fight and use his karate' skills to beat the criminals up.

Even though my grandmother was a church going woman and a prayer warrior, satan had already been at work in my mind. The love and prayers of my grandmother and great-grandmother did not stop me from using my God given talents for destructive behavior instead of good. Soon after I moved in with my grandmother and great-grandmother I began attending Graham Temple Church in North Minneapolis with my grandmother. While she was in service, I was playing craps in the church basement with other children who attended the church.

A church member came downstairs and started fussing at me. She told the pastor, "The devil was somewhere in the church and got a hold of this child!" When my grandmother found out, I got a whuppin' with a paddle. When I tell this story to friends and family, I always joke that's when I felt the board of education.

At age eleven I was in what may be called by some a gang, but they were people I associated with in gang activity. My grandmother and great-grandmother's love, prayers and encouragement did not stop me from robbing a hardware store at gunpoint. A teenager from the neighborhood, Scooby had the guns, so we robbed the hardware store. As Scooby held the gun at the hardware store owner's head. The owner was pleading with us kids not to kill him. The owner who was an older gentleman asked, "Why are you kids doing this?" I thought in that moment he knows we're kids. I saw the power-of-control-look on Scooby's face as he was pushing the hardware store owner to move so he could shoot him. It seemed, as though Scooby was enjoying being able to have life or death at the end of his fingertips.

I was really scared as sweat was running all down my skinny, tall 11-year-old frame. I kept walking around in the store so no one could see how much I was shaking. Because we were about to catch a murder case! That's how much heart I thought Scooby had. He was not playing. The next thing I know we were out the door with a bag full of money.

After the robbery we ran for several blocks into an abandoned garage where the four of us started splitting up the money. We got away with about $86.00 and some change. To celebrate our success of skipping school on a nice mid-summer afternoon and pulling off an armed-robbery we all decided to put our money together and get something from the liquor store.

Because we were not old enough to buy liquor or be in the liquor store, we had to pay any old wino standing out front of the liquor store to go inside and get what we wanted. But when the wino asked us what we wanted to drink we didn't really know what we wanted. So, we told the wino to pick out something good. The wino standing in front of us with the smell alcohol coming from his skin and his breath shuffled away into the liquor store. He looked as though he would tip over and fall at any time. When he returned you wouldn't believe what he bought us. Yeah! You guessed it, a bottle of wine. It came in a green bottle with a white label that read Thunderbird.

Scooby who was about 16 years-old had the highest rank of this group of associates. He took the bottle from the old man and we walked off into the sunset, towards an abandoned garage. Once we were inside, we opened the bottle. Scooby handed me the bottle and told me to take a big hit. He wanted me to hold the bottle and take a big gulp. I did. Then Scooby said, "Hit it again." I held the bottle about an inch away from my nose. Before I even took a gulp, I already smelled the fumes from the alcohol. But the second gulp I took was not as big as the first gulp I took.

The other two guys that were with us started laughing, as I handed Scooby back the bottle. After those two gulps I began to feel the rush of the alcohol immediately going to my head, followed by a short gasp and deep cough. This phase lasted about 30 seconds. I felt extremely light-headed before the wine could even get passed to the rest of the guys. Before the guys got their gulps, I already had my hand out for more. This moment launched my drinking career at the age of 11.

THE KNOCK AT THE DOOR

Do not be deceived: God is not mocked, for whatever one sows, that will he also reap. For the one who sows to his own flesh will from the flesh reap corruption, but the one who sows to the Spirit will from the Spirit reap eternal life. And let us not grow weary of doing good, for in due season we will reap, if we do not give up. So then, as we have opportunity, let us do good to everyone, and especially to those who are of the household of faith.

—Galatians 6:7–10
English Standard Version (ESV)

THE RINGING GOT louder in my mind. I answered the door in my head, not knowing what to expect. Hearing the sound getting louder and louder. There was so much noise in my head, that I couldn't even hear God's whisper. The devil was putting loud and confusing thoughts in my mind to keep on doing wrong. While God was whispering to me about having a choice! I was deep off into the street game now and was getting lessons from the older macks and the ladies of the night.

I remember back in 1967 in Red Wing Correctional Facility in Minnesota, Red Wing had several cottages built for young offenders, the two I remember are Duke Security Cottage and Brown Cottage. Brown Cottage was right next to Duke Cottage. Red Wing looked like the state penitentiary for adults. It was fenced in all around the facility with barbed wire fencing.

The facility was supposedly built to hold young offenders. But when I arrived it only took five days before we (the young offenders) took it over. About twenty-five of us kids started a riot inside Duke Security Cottage. We took over the control room and chased the guards out of the cottage.

We held Duke Cottage down for over twenty-four hours and would only let the Commissioner of the Department of Corrections in to talk to us. The commissioner was telling us that if we did not release the cottage back to the authorities that they would have to use the force of the National Guard. I already knew what the force of the National Guard felt like. Because I already had a run in with the National Guard on the north side of Minneapolis, July 1967 when there was a riot on Plymouth Avenue, stemming from racial tension. Riotous demonstrations were erupting across the nation due to the continued mistreatment of black citizens.

The difference between the 1967 riots across the country and the 2020 riots is mostly Black with a few whites marched and rioted with black people. And riots and marches were predominately in cities (urban areas). The current marches/riots are national, international, Black people, White people, Asian people, Latin people, men, women, and children. Raising their fist as a sign of Black power and fighting against oppression. (Wikipedia, n.d.) notes,

> The black fist, also known as the Black Power Fist a logo generally associated with black nationalism and sometimes socialism. Its most widely known usage is by the

Black Panther Party in the 1960s. A black fist logo was also adopted by the northern soul music subculture.

Back to the riots on Plymouth Avenue.

(MNOPEDIA n.d) writes, On the night of July 19, 1967, racial tension in North Minneapolis erupted along Plymouth Avenue in a series of acts of arson, assaults, and vandalism. The violence, which lasted for three nights, is often linked with other race-related demonstrations in cities across the nation during 1967's "long hot summer."

I was going to Lincoln Junior High School located on Penn Avenue before I got my second bit (time in a juvenile facility) at Red Wing. A lot of us kids was throwing rocks and everything at the Minneapolis Police as buildings on Plymouth Avenue was burning to the ground. My friends and I were on top of one of the buildings throwing rocks at the police. Out of nowhere we started seeing army trucks.

1967 Plymouth Avenue Riots Minneapolis, MN

1967 Plymouth Avenue Riots Minneapolis, MN

1967 Plymouth Avenue Riots Minneapolis, MN

1967 Plymouth Avenue Riots Minneapolis, MN

1967 Plymouth Avenue Riots Minneapolis, MN

1967 Plymouth Avenue Riots Minneapolis, MN

I remember seeing people breaking into stores, running down the street through houses and yards, and people getting beat up by police. As we (my friends and I) were hearing gun shots and seeing tear gas coming from all directions, me and a couple of my friends ran to my grandmother's house for safety.

Like I said before, my grandmother was a praying woman, and I remember her letting us in the door and her getting on her knees to pray. I don't know exactly what she was praying for, but I know us kids were in there somewhere. As daylight approached all you could see when you looked out the window was National Guards on every corner.

You could hear people shouting out their windows as police were cuffing people and taking them away. People were yelling about the curfew placed on north Minneapolis residents. They were saying, "WE'RE NOT ANIMALS!"

Suddenly, I heard a voice getting louder in my head; as the front door to my house opened wider, in my mind; I heard; "Wake Up!" My mind brought me back to listening to the Commissioner of the Department of Corrections at the Red Wing facility talking to us about giving up and letting the Red Wing Guards return to the security cottage. While the commissioner was talking, I noticed the crowd getting smaller as I went to go use the bathroom. I saw kids jumping out of the windows.

Red Wing Correctional Facility

One of the guys from our clique said to me, "Come on Lee, we're breaking out someone made a hole in the fence." Before I knew it, I was outside making my way to the fence with the rest of the kids. There was five of us in our clique. It's funny when I think back on it. Because it was three of us that were Black, one Indian, and the other one Italian. As society would often have people believe it's always Black people doing wrong. We got out of the fence and made our way across Red Wing's highway up to Rattle Snake Bluff.

It was dark now and we could see flashlights down at the bottom of the bluff. We could hear helicopters, but we didn't know if they were looking for us. Kenney was kind of the leader of our clique, even though we were all crazy and had heart. Kenney was providing guidance as we moved through the bluffs. That's why we all got along. When we thought it was safe, we went down the bluff. Believe it or not, they didn't call it Rattle Snake Bluff for nothing.

I think we killed a couple of them with rocks and sticks while we were going through, what seemed like swamps and mud. We wasn't for sure if they were dead, but we didn't stay there to find out. We must've been walking for some time because after a while we saw railroad tracks. I think we walked through poison ivy because everyone was itching and wanted to turn themselves in. We saw a lot of farm-land but we didn't walk through it because we were scared of getting shot. Because we were criminals and runaways.

Even though we were kids, I don't think society even cared. I felt like the slaves did when they were running away from their master. I was not going back to red Wing because we were treated badly. I remember being locked up in Brown Cottage before going to Duke Cottage. They locked you in a room for twenty-four hours with a pot to do your business in (use the bathroom). And they took your mattress out too. In the morning they gave you a brush and had you clean out your own feces from the pot. That's one of the many issues that made us riot.

While walking on the railroad tracks, everyone was getting tired. We thought about going back into the ditch just to lay down and get some rest, but everyone was scared of the rattlesnakes. We thought they were coming to get us because we knocked out their snake partners. Something only a kid would think of. Just then, Geino, the Italian kid, said; "Look!" Next to the railroad tracks there was an old '62 Ford. Low and behold, there were keys in the car.

The was only one problem with finding the car, only two of us knew how to drive. Kenney who was Black and Robert who was Indian. Letting a Black kid drive in a White people town like Red Wing, Minnesota in 1964 would have us back at Duke Cottage before we could even get the car started. So, we let Robert drive and Geino sit in the front seat because they both looked White. And to get out of Red Wing we needed to drive through the small town in this '62 Ford. The rest of us, who were darker in skin color laid down in the backseat.

I fell asleep dreaming and thinking that the police pulled us over and took us somewhere to beat us and hang us from trees. I also dreamt they would beat up the White kid, the worst for being with kids of color. While dreaming and thinking I was awakened by sounds of trucks on the highway. I sat up to see bright lights. Even though I didn't know it, God and his angels must've been watching over us because that old Ford car made it all the way to the south side of Minneapolis on Franklin Avenue, about 70 miles, before it completely stopped on us.

We didn't know if it ran out of gas or what. We was going to have to get out and walk or steal another car. We had to make it over north to my grandma's house. I told them that we were better off on foot making it to the north side of Minneapolis. We could lay low for a day or so. I knew from past experience it was going to take a couple of days for the authorities to get a hold of all the kids' who broke out of Red Wing. Because all those kids' probation officers would have to be contacted.

We made it over to north Minneapolis from the south side of Minneapolis by walking on Nicollet Avenue to Loring Park through downtown to Lyndale. Once on Lyndale Avenue to Glenwood Avenue, we went from Glenwood to Highway 55 (Olson Memorial Highway). My grandmother and great-grandmother lived in a big white house on James Avenue North right around the corner from Highway 55.

The rest of the gang followed me up to my grandmother's front steps. As I started knocking on the door, I heard someone say, "Who is it?" I said, "It's me grandmom, Lee!" My grandmom said, "Who? You kids get away from the door. Lee is in jail." I said, "No it's me, Lee!" But this time in a loud voice. It was daylight so she opened the door. When she saw me and the guys she looked surprised and relieved at the same time. The first thing that came out of my grandmom's mouth was, "You all can't stay here. We saw and heard on the news about a bunch of kids breaking out of jail."

I told my grandmom everything that had happen to us in Red Wing and how we was being treated. My great-grandmom got up from her rocking chair and went to the kitchen. She was glad to see me. I said mama we just want to lay on the living room floor for a while and get some sleep. She looked at my great-grandmother. My great-grand-mother said, "Let the child and his friends stay awhile." The next thing I knew, my grandmom gave us wash cloths to clean up with. She took our shirts and socks to wash them. She told us by the time our clothes dry, that was hanging on the back porch, we would have to leave.

My friends gave the most respect to my grandparents. And when the food was put on the table, we was truly grateful to God. It felt like we had not ate or drank anything in years. When all five of us boys laid down on that living room floor to get some sleep, I know the gang must have felt the same way I did. We was laying on a mattress from heaven. I could hear my grandmother in the kitchen singing and praying as I was falling into a deep sleep. While drifting off to sleep I thought about the knock at the door. Looking back, I believe I was already wanting to understand How can we so selfishly become Dead in our mind. To want to stop Living in our hearts.

RUN LITTLE GANGSTER RUN

"And to the angel of the church in Philadelphia write: 'The words of the holy one, the true one, who has the key of David, who opens and no one will shut, who shuts and no one opens.

—Revelation 3:7

Put no trust in extortion; set no vain hopes on robbery; if riches increase, set not your heart on them.

—Psalm 62:10
English Standard Version (ESV)

IT FELT LIKE the boys and myself must have slept for years on my grandmother and great-grandmother's living room floor. But it was only hours that passed, as reality settled back in with our noses being awakened by the sweet smell of bacon and pancakes. My grandmother told us to go and wash our hands and get dressed. Grandma had washed our socks and shirts and they were now dry on the back porch.

Now with all of us boys sitting at the table ready to eat and my grandmother saying grace (prayer), I knew she was praying for us because she kept praying for God to watch over the children. And protect all the children while they go on the journey. What journey? I thought to myself. I did not know it at the time, but she was talking about life's journey. My thoughts was interrupted by all the laughing at the table from the guys. How happy they was to be eating a great meal. They gave my grandmother credit on how great a cook she was. It made my grandmother smile as well as my great-grandmother who just got of her rocking chair and was passing by the dining room.

Then my grandmother said in a serious; caring voice, "They were talking about you boys on the news again. You're going to have to get ready to leave our home now Lee. But I want to talk to you for a moment." I followed my grandmother to her bedroom where she picked up her bible, opened to a page, and gave me $20 dollars. When I was a kid, older people would always keep important things tucked in between the pages of their bibles. Even today I sometimes wonder if grandma gave me her weekly church tithe (money to the church). She looked at me with tears in her eyes. Tears that I could see through the wet smear in her eye-glasses. I told her, I love her, and I miss my mom. And I asked her if she would let my mom know I was alright.

In that moment I felt the great overwhelming love my grandmother must have had for me and my mom. It almost made me want to cry. And when I think about that moment even now, I feel that same, overwhelming feeling. I also felt my grandmother must have been going through a lot taking care of her one and only child. My mom who was 14 years old when she became pregnant with me and my grandmother was taking care of the both of us. All of those, memories came to mind. That's probably why I was missing my mom as well. You cannot have better protection than a grandmother's prayer or beat a grandmother's love.

I could have called my mom from my grandparent's house, but I thought they might have my mom's phone bugged (wiretap). I guess in my young little mind I felt the crew and I had done something notorious by breaking out of Red Wing. My thoughts went back to what my grandmother was saying to me. I did know that the next words she spoke to me would stay with me for the rest of my life. She said, "Lee, you are my grandson and regardless, what people think about you, if God is for you who can be against you. Remember, Lee there is a fork in the road, and you will have to choose."

My grandmother walked away from me, going back to join the others in the dining room. She gave Kenney a bag full of sandwiches as we all gave hugs, kisses, and goodbyes. My grandmother thought we had left her house, but the five of us were in the garage in the backyard so we could figure out our next move. Walter and Kenney spoke up first. We need to steal another car. Then I thought about what my grandmother said about the fork in the road, I spoke up and said, "I am not going back to the joint. And we need a lot of money to leave town. No one knows what we look like; but the police. I have some friends on both sides of town that we can trust."

Kenney started to argue with me. Geino and Robert agreed with me. Kenney backed down and now I became the leader. I said, "Let's go. The bus we need to get there will be coming, soon." They followed me to the open streets. No words were spoken as the five of us sat at the but stop. And no words were needed. Our loyalty for each other was there. And I knew, I was now on the path to the forked road but was not choosing the path my grandmother would want me to take, and there was no turning back. We was all about to become some Bad Little Gangsters.

As the bus pulled up to the bus stop, we got on and took a seat. We needed to travel to the other side of North Minneapolis where my grandfather lived. The ride was not long but it was fascinating to Geino. He was from New York originally. Geino had only seen Minneapolis while passing through to other states. Looking out the bus window I think he was thinking about home. When we got to my grandfather's apartment, he welcomed us in with open arms.

He told me my mom and grandmother had called him and told him me and some kids had broke out of the joint. I told my grandfather a lie, I said some other gang was after us and we needed to protect ourselves. And I knew he could get us some guns. My grandfather said to me, "You bad little kids can't even hold a gun let alone carry one. And where would you get the money?" "We'll pay you back with interest" I said. I also told my grandfather, "The gang and I are going to do a robbery so we can have some money to leave town." I lied to my grandfather again.

My grandfather worked a job, but he was still a well-known hustler. And he knew how to get things. Him and my grandmother broke up because he got drunk a lot and she started going to church. The rest of the guys was standing next to me as I started to introduce my friends to my grandfather. He just looked at us and said, "So you want to be little gangsters. Meet me in the back of the parking lot. I am going to take you young thugs for a little ride." We did as we was told, and got into a 1965 green Cadillac convertible. The ride maybe lasted about a ½ hour. During the ride we was sitting in the car listening to some colorful jazz on my grandfather's radio.

We ended up coming to a stop on Golden Valley Road at a gun shop. I got out of the car with my grandfather while the others stayed put. The white guy must have knew my grandfather because they started talking about the old days. Then the white guy said to my grandfather, "What can I do for you or help you with today? Remember I still owe you one for saving my life." Regarding saving the white guy's life, my grandfather stopped some guys from killing him. I don't know the whole story I just know the guys who wanted to kill him had the wrong guy. And my grandfather told them they had the wrong guy. So, the white guy was grateful.

My grandfather said to him, "Don't know if you remember my nice Willa Mae, this is her son Lee. Him and his friends want to protect themselves from some other B-A-D kids wanting to play tough with them. You know what I mean?" Grandfather put one of his hands up in the air and said, "I need five cap pistols and some rolls of caps. Who knows they might want to play cowboys without riding horses.

The people on the street called my grandfather, gangster mole. I guess 'cause he did a lot of strong arming back in his days and went underground. My grandfather and I left out of the gun shop empty-handed, as he waved goodbye to the white guy. We both got back into the Cadillac and to my surprise the man came running out of the store and said to my grandfather, "Hey! Hey! You forgot your bag and receipt." I never saw a transaction between my grandfather or the gun shop man. But when we got back to my grandfather's apartment, he took the merchandise out of the bag. The white guy showed my grandfather his gratitude for saving his life by helping me and my crew out.

There sitting on his table was three, twenty-two revolvers; two, twenty-five automatics and a box of shells for each gun. I grabbed the one with the white pearl handle. Kenney grabbed the twenty-two revolver. And Robert picked up the other twenty-two. Geino had no complaints picking up one of the pearl handle automatics. While we could see Walter mumbling under his breath, as he picked up other the other automatic, which looked small in his huge hand. I guess he thought with his short, black, stocky frame and nappy hair that the gun was too small for him.

By this time, the gang and I had already been involved in some interesting situations.

Some of the guys I knew before I got to Red Wing. Some I met at Red Wing. I knew Walter could fight. I seen him take on a couple of kids in the joint. Me, with my tall lanky brown light-skin self, had a reputation of stabbing folks. They heard about what I did to a bully kid in school trying to take my lunch money. Robert the Indian kid who could pass for white, had the reputation of sneaking up on people. He was quiet but dangerous!

Some kid had threatened him in the joint. Robert had gotten into the kid's room that night and set his bed on fire; with him in it! That's how he wound up in Duke Security Cottage at Red Wing with the rest of us. Kenney was a little bit shorter than I was. He was brown skinned and just as stocky as Walter. But his hair was not nappy. I guess 'cause me and Kenny kept Jap in our hair. Jap was a process (relaxer) you put in your hair to straighten out the naps and kinks.

I knew Kenny had heart, cause we robbed and strong-armed together at one time or another. But we never hung out till now. Geino, the Italian kid with his small frame had black hair and green eyes. His features almost made him look like a choir boy. But he was far from that. He was in the joint for assault with a deadly weapon, for taking some kid's eye out. We became friends in the lumber camp where we spent a short time.

I liked little Geino. We was tee-heeing and laughing at Walter as he was showing Geino how well the twenty-five automatic fit in his hand. My grandfather was in the bedroom talking to someone, I think was his girlfriend. Either she wasn't there before, or we just didn't see her. My grandfather must have asked her to fix us a drink and give us something to eat. Then my grandfather said we was going to have to leave in a little while.

He told me to call my mama. He said, "Boy there ain't no phone tap on your mom's phone." My mom was glad to hear from me. But I think it made me feel more, lonely at the same time. For a moment, my thoughts went back to my first robbery at age eleven, at the hardware store. The store-clerk had this look on his face that he was about to die! As Scooby held the gun at the clerk's head.

My thought was interrupted by my grandfather handing me some money, while taking a glass of liquor from Kenney's hand saying, "You little thugs ain't getting drunk in my house." I knew my grandfather was getting tired of showing us, his hospitality. We put some shells in our pockets and the rest of the bullets in the paper brownbag full of sandwiches my grandmother had gave us. I was telling the gang about a drugstore on Lake Street, on the south side of Minneapolis. The drugstore had three cash registers and no security inside. Geino wanted to rob a bank, but then said what the heck money is money.

I asked grandfather after we pull a job, did he know a place we could stay at for a while? He said, "No! You all get the f*&% out of here." I thanked my grandfather and told him we would pay him back soon for all he did for us. He just waved his hand goodbye and said, "Now if the police get behind you, don't stop running. They will shoot you standing still. So, you better run. Run little gangsters run!" I thought to myself on many occasions, MY LORD GOD, PLEASE FORGIVE US KIDS. FOR WE DID NOT KNOW WHAT WE WAS REALLY DOING!

As the five of us was walking to the bus stop, I saw a white four door Buick pass by us and do a u-turn. The car started honking the horn as it pulled along beside us. "Hey Lee! When you get out? And where you cats, goin'?" It was Zero, a Lincoln Junior High School friend of mine. He knew when I went to the joint for a stolen car. The thing about that was I didn't even know how to drive! Talk about being railroaded! "Where did you get the cool car?" I asked Zero. He said it was a friend of his. I knew Zero to lie, but I didn't care. We needed a ride. It would stop us from transferring on to three buses.

I told Zero they let me out two days ago for good behavior, and I ran into the rest of guys over in Saint Paul. I asked Zero would he like to make some gas money by taking us over to South Minneapolis. He signaled all of us to get in. As we got into the car Zero looked at me and said, "Where you goin' with that pistol?" He must of saw it while I was getting into the front seat. I asked Zero if he wanted in on the robbery, we was about to pull on the drug store over south. And all he had to do was wait around the corner in the back of the alley? Zero agreed, and we was on our way.

RUN LITTLE GANGSTER RUN THE CHASE! PART 2

ZERO PULLED UP to the front of the drug store. This was the moment we all was waiting for! Four of us was going in, while Walter stood outside being the look-out. To show you how bold we was we did not have on any masks or anything! We knew what we was gonna do and by golly we was gonna do it! We went in the store like the gangsters we was. Not caring who was in the store. Robert stood inside the store, gun in hand. While I pointed to Geino and Kenney to show them where the other two cash registers was, when I heard screaming, I knew they was at the registers.

I was at the front register saying, "I don't want to hurt you, but I will!" I shouted, "Put all the money in this sock! That's Right!" I said, "Sock!" I knew they didn't stink cause my grandmother had just washed them. And they was Red Wing socks so I knew they was strong. The lady was scared. As she was putting the money in my sock I was scared as well. But did not show it. As the adrenaline was running through my little body I was keeping it real (keeping it 100). While we all were at cash registers people had their hands in the air. I was surprised that nobody tried to run to the door.

It seemed like a long time in the store, but it had not even been four minutes. Kenney, Geino, and I were coming to the front of the store with our socks in our hands. The drugstore door flew open. With a loud shout Walter, our look-out yelled, "They're coming up the street!" Walter didn't know he almost got shot by Geino and Robert. Funny, I thought. 'Cause we did not hear no police sirens. But he was right! We all ran out the store the drug store. We was on the corner because it was the quickest way to get to the alley.

We was all running like we was running for our lives. When we got in the alley to our surprise, Zero was gone. We could hear the sirens now! "Halt! Halt! You black so and so!" As the police were yelling I could hear sirens, yelling and the whistle of bullets going past our heads! The police was yelling, "Put your hands up!" I could hear the screeching of tires as whistling bullets continued flying past us and ripping through trash cans. We were running through houses now to get away from the police. It seemed like the policemen's voices and gun shots was fading away. But we kept on running!

While running I was praying to Jesus and God over and over. I thought about what my grandfather said, "Keep on running little gangsters." My thoughts was interrupted by Kenney asking me, "What now?" We was standing on the side of a garage taking a breather. Dogs were barking from everywhere. I saw a high school and remembered a girl I use to like lived on the other side of the school. She had two other sisters and her mom lived there.

Carol's mom was religious and even though she knew I was, quote; considered a bad kid who's been in jail and foster homes, neither she or her family ever judged me. I told the gang if we could just make it to Carol's house, we could figure out our next move. But their house was still several blocks away. I don't know how the five of us made it to Carol's, mom's house without getting caught. But I know now. God was watching over us kids all the time, even though we was doing wrong. When we got to the porch, I told the gang to stay back.

Geino was still talking about killing Zero for leaving us. The rest of us was upset for leaving our bag of food and shells in Zero's, friend's car. The only thing that was going our way right now was, we had three socks full of money. So far, we had gotten away with armed-robbery. As the door opened I saw Alice's smiling face. Behind her was Carol's younger sister Punkin. They was glad to see me, as well as I was to see them. I introduced the sisters to the rest guys who was already smacking their lips and thinking about which one of the sisters they was going to bang first.

I knew even though they was all young teens, the end result with these sisters is the gang's feelings was goin' to be hurt. 'Cause Carol and I broke up because she wasn't puttin' out nothin' but a kiss. Then her and her mom was always trying to drag me to church. I asked where Carol and her mom was at? One of the sisters answered, "Mama and Carol went shopping and then they're going on to church." I just smiled and asked if we can come in for a while. The sisters said, "Okay." We asked if we could use the bathroom.

The first thing that came out of Alice's mouth was, "I am telling our mama if me and Punkin don't get a cut! It was you guys they been talking about on the news! Any time all five of you want to use the bathroom at the same time, something's up!" Then she looked at Robert and Geino and started laughing. She said, "You two ain't even Black!"

The gang agreed to give Punkin and Alice $50 each, even though we didn't know how much we had. All of us went up to the big bathroom the sister's, had in their house. We dumped the money from the socks on the floor and divvied the money between us. After giving the sisters their cut, we had about $270.00 a, piece. We paid Punkin to go get us some chicken while Alice let us take a short nap. I slept but did not rest. I woke up looking at the others feeding their faces.

I told Alice that we had to get back on the northside, and for another $50 each would they help us. It was now getting late and we had did a lot in the past forty-eight hours. I wanted to get high and take a hot bath somewhere. I told the guys that we needed to split up and meet at Old Henry Hamburger joint over north. I told Robert and Geino to take a cab with Punkin. I told Kenney and Walter to take the bus to Cliff Café down the street from the hamburger place. Then I told them me and Alice will take a cab and meet you at Cliff's.

The gang didn't want to split up. I said, "If push comes to shove, you know where my grandmother lives. You need trust I know what I am doing." The truth was I really didn't know, but I didn't want them still here in Carol's, mom's house in case they came home from church and heard about the robbery. Everything went as planned. We all met at Cliff's Café. It felt good to see the whole crew. For some reason we felt strong, powerful, and unstoppable when we were together.

There was a lot of pimps, hustlers, ladies of the night, and older people that hung out at the café. There were even some old-timers that I know, knew my grandfather. They didn't care a bunch of young teens was hanging out late. Punkin said while at the hamburger place, her aunt was there, and told her that they caught one of the armed robbers in a stolen green car. And said he must have been the ring-leader 'cause he had bullets, ammo (ammunition) and food in the car when the police stopped him. We all started laughing, except Geino. Alice smiled remembering the news said they were looking for a bunch of black kids as she's looking at one young man who's Indian and another young man who's Italian.

We said goodbye to the sisters. I said, "Will you tell your mom to keep us in prayer." Alice said you know what our mama will tell you Lee, "I will pray for you all, but you all should be ashamed of yourselves. Someone could have gotten hurt, or even killed." Then Punkin said mama would tell you Lee, "All money, ain't good money. Give your young hearts to Jesus." I looked at the two sisters and said, "Look who's talking, didn't you all just take a hundred bucks of no good money?" "That's not the point." One sister said. "You little gangsters needed our help! And you're on the run! But remember you can't hide from the most-high. So run! You little, pistol-packing gangsters run!" They smiled and blew us a kiss as they got on the bus and left.

AIN'T NUTHIN' SHAKIN'
BUT THE BACON

Let your hand be ready to help me, for I have chosen your precepts.

—Psalm 119:176
English Standard Version (ESV)

AS THE BUS pulled off with Alice and Punkin we all went back into the café' and ordered something to eat. Even though we was not that hungry we just needed a place to sit and rest. Just then my grandfather's girlfriend and some other lady walked into the café. She immediately saw us sitting in the café booth. One of the waitresses called my grandfather's girlfriend by her name. The waitress said, "C.C. do you know these youngsters?" C.C. replied, "Yes I do." While looking directly at me, walking towards our table and signaling her friend she came to the café with to save her a seat at the counter.

I said, "Hi C.C. have you seen my grandfather? We was going to stop by." Before another word came out of my mouth C.C. interrupted me and said, "What are you little gangsters up to now? No! Heck No! You little gangsters are not bringing your little butts back over there!

You know what your grandfather said. He ain't seen you and don't want to be you." I said, "C.C. I just wanted to ask again if he knew a place we could stay." C.C. was nice and said she would give us a hook up. Hook up meaning, she would help us. I just had to promise not to tell my grandfather.

She said we could use her girlfriend's place. The girlfriend who was sitting at the café counter waiting on her. C.C. said she would let her friend T.T. know what was going on. C.C. shared she had to get out on the Plymouth Avenue strip but T.T. would take us where we needed to go. C.C. brought T.T. over to the booth we were sitting at and introduced all of us (the guys and myself). As C.C. was leaving, she looked back at us smiled and said, "Did you know somebody robbed the drugstore over in south Minneapolis?" Before she walked out the café door. I thought to myself, dang Minneapolis is just too dang small of a city.

We felt a relief come over us because we was going to have a place to stay for tonight. I asked the waitress to bag up our food, we hadn't even touched it. I think we was all hanging on C'C.'s every word. T.T. was cool and was just as fine as C.C. T.T. told us we was in good hands. T.T. said she was going to take us to a rooming house here on the northside to meet a man called Shakin' Bacon. T.T. smiled at all of us as the waitress brought back our food all bagged up. We all got up from the table and left the café.

T.T. knew a lot of people on the Plymouth Avenue Strip. Guys in their cars was whistling and honking at her. One of them even asked her where she was going with a bunch of little tricks. T.T. just gave him the finger and kept on walking. Geino was getting mad and said to me in a low voice, "That cat will get a couple of caps in his behind if he gets out of his car and comes across the street." I know Geino was not playin'. He would of shot the man. I took Geino's mind off the man by telling him to walk up front with the rest of the guys who were talking with T.T. Seeing that we had already walked several blocks, I asked her how many blocks we had to go.

T.T. came back to where I was and pointed to a brown looking house around the corner. As we was approaching the steps of the house two ladies of the night was leaving the house. I knew what they were from my experience staying in a rooming house in Detroit. I also knew this was more than a plain old rooming house. We was met at the door by a huge stocky framed black man who's skin was so black it almost looked purple. His stone-cold eyes seemed to stare right through you.

T.T. walked up to the man and said, "Shakin' Bacon this my nephew Lee and his friends. Their parents worked far out at a warehouse in Saint Paul. My nephew and his parents carpooled together and the car broke down. They won't get back until real late. I promise my sister I would look after them till morning." I thought to myself, Wow. If they was giving out an Oscar Award for the best lie, T.T. would get it. She was good.

Shakin' Bacon talked real fast. With a serious look on his face, he looked at T.T. and said, "Ain't Nuthin' Shakin' In my House but The Bacon. I am standing here with my hand out! Why Is It Still Shakin'?" T.T went into her bra and put some money in his hand, smiled, and signaled us kids to follow her up to her room. I saw out the corner of my eye a .38 pistol up under Shakin' Bacon's shirt. I knew right then he was nothin' to play with. So, I told the gang to be cool while we was T.T.'s guests. Shakin' Bacon was still talking stuff to T.T. as we was going up the stairs his voice got quieter as we entered T.T's room, and she shut the door.

T.T. said, "Don't pay attention to Shakin' Bacon. He a good guy. He just like to keep his other ladies in check. So, he pretends I'm one of the ladies in his stable so that I can keep the room. I'm an outlaw." What kind of an outlaw?" Asked Robert. Even though I knew I kept my mouth shut. My Aunt Charlene who I lived with in Detroit had a couple of outlaws living in her building. T.T. told Robert that she did not have no man. And she's not giving no player her hard-working street money. So the streets saw her as an outlaw.

While their conversation was going on, I was checking out the room. It had a bathroom, a small hot plate an ice box in the corner of the room, and a small sink in the other corner of the room. There was a couch and chair with a coffee table that had a radio on it. There was also another little chair that had a broken leg. T.T. saw me and the others looking around while she was talking to Robert. I thought to myself another night of sleeping on the floor as I watched a couple of roaches already making camp by the end of the coffee table. T.T. then went over to what looked like a china cabinet and to my surprise pulled a bed out of the wall (a murphy bed).

T.T. said the sheets are clean cause I keep them that way for my friend. I told the gang to fork over ten dollars each. I gave it to T.T. for coming out of her pocket with Shakin' Bacon. She looked at me and said, "Your so sweet. You're going to go far in the pimp game when you grow up." Believe it or not I didn't have a clue what T.T. was talking about. I liked money too much to sit around and wait to get paid when I could just take it. Geino was already in the shower.

Kenney was trying to find something on the radio. Walter and Robert was sitting on the couch eating some of the food we brought with us from Cliff Café.

T.T. said she would see us in the morning and told us to stay in the room. She needed to go to work. Yes, ladies of the night had to find men who would pay them for a good time. These men were called tricks or marks. And the ladies had to work the streets to get paid. I fell back on the bed. Wow! We had money in our pockets, a place to sleep, good food, and everyone was just happy to take a shower.

I laid there on the bed and fell into a deep sleep. I was awakened by some guy and lady talking in the hallway. Kenney, Walter, Robert, and Geino was knocked out in a deep sleep like I was. I got up from the bed, drunk a cup of water, ate a few bites of my cold hamburger and fries, and got into the shower. It wasn't quite morning yet. I got out of the shower and got dressed. I was listening to the radio to try and figure out what time it was. With the guys snoring it was hard to hear the radio. But I knew they was just as tired as I was.

I sat on the edge of the bed thinking about our next move. I thought about the gang in Detroit, The Black Stone Rangers. I remember being told by a lieutenant from this gang, "If we didn't corner our block, the block would corner us; police included.". I was too young at the time to know exactly what he meant. However, much of the work this gang did initially was protecting the community of Detroit from police brutality. As the gang grew it turned into more of criminal enterprise then community protection.

A quick note about the Black Stone Rangers. (Curry 2010)

> The Blackstone Rangers were founded by two teenagers, Jeff Fort and Eugene Hairston while they were at the Illinois School for Boys in St. Charles. In it's earliest days the Rangers were mostly local neighborhood kids who banded together for protection against rival gangs. Their intentions however began to expand as the gang turned to profitable criminal activity. By 1965, the Blackstone Rangers ballooned to 5,000 members.

My mind was racing once again and returned to the current situation. I was a little gangster on the run. My gang was depending on me. I know we needed new clothes and shoes. Maybe we should rob a clothing store. I felt good with the rest I had. I heard the birds chirping as the sunlight started coming through the little window in the room. As I looked out, I saw the alleyway and house rooftops.

My thoughts was interrupted by a key turning in the door. It was T.T. coming in. Before she could close the door good I could hear Shakin' Bacon's voice telling T.T., "Get those little thugs out of my house!" The rest of the gang got up and got themselves together. We gave T.T. a few more dollars for helping us out. Shakin' Bacon was at the end of the stairs yelling, "T.T. I knew you and these little gangsters was fakin'. That's why my hand is still shakin'".

T.T walked us outside. We all reached in our pocket and gave Shakin' Bacon another five dollars. Then he smiled at us and gave us back our five dollars. I asked T.T. why he gave us back our money. The others didn't care, I was just curious. T.T. said he has tremors (a quivering that makes a person shake). T.T. said "Lee maybe he thought you seen him shakin'." As an adult I found out Shakin' Bacon had the same disease Muhammad Ali had, Parkinson's.

IF YOU CAN SAY HUH?
YOU CAN HEAR

"Hear my prayer, O Lord, and give ear to my cry; hold not your peace at my tears! For I am a sojourner with you, a guest, like all my fathers.

—Psalm 39:12
English Standard Version (ESV)

The Lord heard me without me not knowing it at the time as a kid

—Rev. Ed Roy

AS WE STEPPED out into sunlight while walking back toward Plymouth Avenue the crisp air was going through my body I could hear the birds chirping, the buses and cars racing past us like they were in a hurry to get to work, we was all in a pretty good mood. Kenny suggested that we stop and get something to eat at one of the little stores down the street. We all got some chips, candy bars, and pop.

Let me share some background information about Plymouth Avenue. Plymouth Avenue in the 1960's was a juxtaposition of different things a strip for the hustlers, players, and ladies of the evening; a place of business as many businesses located on Plymouth Avenue before the riots were owned by Black people and Jewish people. Minneapolis residents who lived in north Minneapolis often share with younger people you never had to go downtown for anything because everything was right here in north Minneapolis.

However, after the 1967 riots Jewish families moved to the suburbs and never reopened their businesses and Black people did not have the financing to rebuild and reopen their businesses. But the riots did bring forth a plan created by north Minneapolis community leaders, community activists, and businessmen to establish a place where young people could hang out in a safe place and community residents could take classes offered by the center. This new neighborhood recreation center was called The Way located at 1913 Plymouth Avenue North. The Way was used and visited by everyone in north Minneapolis. But sadly, The Way is now gone and was replaced by a police station, the Fourth Precinct.

The Way Minneapolis, MN Plymouth Avenue

Getting back to the story, I had already planned for us to go to a clothing store today and buy some things. Geino wanted us to rob a bank first. This cat had bank on his mind. Geino was trigger happy. I thought he maybe was trying to make a name for himself. I flipped Geino's thoughts by saying, "I know of a clothing and shoe store in a little mall on Olson Highway called Thom McAnn Shoes and the V Store. We can get some new clothes then go downtown. The rest agreed so we got on the bus and headed for the V Store.

As we walked into the clothing store a lady's voice came from behind the counter saying, "Oh No You Didn't Come In Here To Rob Me!" I said, "Huh?" while looking at Mrs. B in the face. I knew Mrs. B's kids from school. She looked at all five of us and said, "If you can huh, then you can hear." I said, "Mrs. B these are friends of mine and we just wanted to buy some clothes." I went to show her some money. She waved her hand and held out a store bag, she said, "Put all your guns, knives, and whatever else you have in this bag. Then you can shop. Or get out. I will give you your guns back when you leave out my store." Mrs. B was part of the fabric of the northside community that worked hard, fought for their community, raised their children, and knew the streets. Just when you think you bad, Mrs. B is going to show you she's grown folk out here.

The guys hesitated at first. But then they listened when they saw me put my gun in the bag. I liked Mrs. B. I knew she was no joke. She meant what she said. Instead of us being some runaway gangsters we would have been some hop-a-long kids, cause Mrs. B would not of had any problem putting a cap in our behinds.

It was a good feeling putting on some fresh new duds. While looking in the dressing room mirror I forgot how old and handsome I looked. Now all I needed was new shoes to match my new black and brown outfit. I know the rest of the guys felt the same way I did. They come out the dressing room looking like different people. I asked Mrs. B if we could put our clothes in a bag. She smiled while putting our guns back in the bag with our clothes. We paid and gave her a little more just for being nice to us.

I wonder sometime why she did not turn us in. I think Mrs. B had compassion for us kids and knew how the police was treating us kids. She also knew how whites was treating us; black kids, men, and women in our northside community. Yes, racism was alive and well in the 60's and 70's. We walked down a few doors past The Hole. The Hole was a teenage club where a lot of black youth went. Where a lot of black youth attended dance parties and hung out. The Thomas McAnn shoe store we was going to was right next door.

We went into the store and came out steppin' in some brand new 'kix', (shoes).

I remember a fence a red fence that separated the housing projects from the shopping center. There was a green dumpster back there where we could get rid of our old clothes safely. We took the bus downtown and got off on Hennepin Avenue, which in the daytime looked like Harlem, New York with all the trimmings. You had the Moby Dick's Club, Schindler's Book Store and Newspaper Stand, Bob's Hat Shop, Market Barbecue, Brown's Clothing Store, Kiefer's Clothing, Bill's Sports Game Room, Forum Café, The great Northern Grocery Store, and Hotel Andrews. Just to name a few. Hennepin Avenue was the ladies of the night and day strip.

Downtown Minneapolis, MN

Downtown Minneapolis, MN

Downtown Minneapolis, MN

Downtown Minneapolis, MN

It was also a pimps, gangsters, and hustlers paradise as well. Kenny and Walter said they was getting hungry. Geino still wanted to know where the bank was. Robert and I agreed with Kenny and Walter. Let's eat! Geino was upset that he was out voted but he felt better when he saw the Form Café'. Food was laid out as cafeteria workers helped us as we walked past their service station with our trays and picked out whatever we wanted to eat.

While sitting at the table I told the gang that we should go over to South Minneapolis and hit (rob) another store. I reminded Geino the bank has guards and it will be harder to get away like we did at the drug store. I did say we could still check it out. The only problem I didn't like was the idea of wearing masks. We would only hit one teller. And we would all go out (leave the building) together. They agreed. So, after we ate, we called a cab and headed over south. My reason for going out south was that I may get a chance to see my mom.

While in the cab suddenly, Geino pulled out his gun and pointed it at the cab driver. It took the rest of us by surprise. Kenny was up in the front seat. I quickly said, "Right on Geino." I had the same idea. I knew we would need a getaway car after we hit the store. Kenny had his gun out and was telling the cab driver to pull over 'cause he knew something was about to happen. Geino said, "We can use this car for the bank job." Geino was getting out of hand and I had to regain control quickly.

I felt a murder was coming. I said, "Geino we need the cab and the driver. Didn't you see that big supermarket back there calling our name?" "Let's hit that." I said. "Then right to the bank." I said to Walter, "You stay with the cab." I also told Walter, "Keep the keys so when you see us coming out of the store let the cab driver go. Tell the cab driver to run and don't look back." Walter understood my words. Geino was losing it. And I know he just wanted to kill somebody. Things went as planned. We hit four of the check counters and used the carry out food bags to carry the money. While running back to the cab we saw the cab driver running. Walter started to shoot at the driver as he (the cab driver) dodged bullets and ducked between some buildings to get away.

I said, "Come on let's get out of here." Robert jumped into the cab driver seat and the rubber tires were screeching so loud when we took off the sound was hurting my ears. Geino asked Walter what happened. Walter said he heard screaming coming from the store. He turned around, looked, and saw us coming. Walter said he only took his eyes off the cab driver for a few seconds. I told myself when I get a chance I would let Walter know I owe him one. But I believe the secret he and I shared saved that cab driver's life. The secret being Walter and I discussed letting the cab driver go.

As we were speeding down the street, we could hear the police sirens. It's funny I looked out the car window and saw Franklin Avenue. The area where the car we stole in Red Wing, when we broke out of Red Wing Correctional Facility broke down. We had bags of money. I told the gang we needed to split up and meet back over in North Minneapolis at Old Henry's Hamburger Shop.

Robert stopped the car in the alley. We got out, gave some money from the armed robbery to Kenny, and put what money we could into our pockets. As we walked out of the alley together and started going our separate ways I saw the police car coming up the street.

Something told me to toss my gun into the bushes. I was glad I did. The police started following me. I went up to a house and stood on the porch, like I lived there. Another police car pulled up from the alley way. They hollered out to me with their guns drawn, "Put Your Hands Up You Little #@&%!" I said, "Is there a problem officers?" With my hands held high. While standing there I remembered how good I thought T.T.'s lie was to Shakin Bacon. I said, "Mr. policeman are you going to keep me out here long? I need to get back in my house soon before my parents come home. I just came outside for a walk and to get some fresh air."

The police started whispering to one another. Then they started laughing out loud. They pointed at me and told me to look at the house window. There were four white faces looking at me as if I had stole something from them. The police said some kids had been robbing stores with guns. They asked me, "Do you know anything about that?" I am upset now because I got caught. So, I said to the officer, "Don't my parents have to be present before I answer any questions because I am underage."

One of the officers started smiling as he was putting me into the car. The officer replied, "Yes, we can have your parents that was looking at you on their porch come down. Now what is your name kid?" I gave my brother's name to the officer. The police car ride was long. They took me back to the store that was just robbed. I also saw the white cab driver outside the store talking to the police. One of the policemen pointed to the car I was sitting in. The cab driver looked at me and shook his head no. The policemen got back in the car and we was on our way downtown to the courthouse and then the juvenile center.

The police told me even though I was not identified, yet; they still needed to keep me because I had over $400.00 in my pocket. When we got inside the courthouse the police seated me on a bench and hand-cuffed me to the bench while they went inside an office. They called my mom and told her I might have been involved in a robbery but their going to probably let me go home with her. They just needed to ask me some questions. The police came out in the hallway and told me that my mother was on her way downtown to get me. They said, 'Ricky all we want you to do is answer a few questions when your mom gets here."

I really didn't care what the police was talking about. I was in deep thought. I was thinking about my gang. Why didn't the cab driver turn me in? And if the others got away? I heard a voice in my head, WAKE UP! My thoughts were interrupted by a policeman coming down the courthouse hallway. He stopped in front of me. He said, "Lee, is that you?" I looked at the officer and said, "No!" The officer came closer and said, "You are Lee." He went into the office and brought out another police officer. He said, "This is Lee. He is one of the boys who escaped from Red Wing Correctional Facility!"

While they was talking my mom was coming down the hall. They told my mom I was not going anywhere. They told my mom I had lied and used my brother's name and other charges may be coming. The police said she could see me for a few minutes then they would be tak-ing me back to Red Wing. I was happy to see my mom. I was mad I got caught. I was angry with the cop that told on me.

BARBED WIRE FENCE
IN THE SKY

You beat me down with hate, but on His word I will stand. The love in my heart will not turn into your hate, you can take my body, lock it up, till it messes with my mind. But I will not give up my soul, you can't have it, your too late, it already belongs to the most High. My grandmother and others saw to it that were praying for me when I did not know how to pray for myself.

—Rev. Ed Roy

DUE TO RUNNING away from Thistledew Camp and Red Wing, and the armed robbery sprees you've been on, the Board of Commission is recommending you go to Lino Lakes Building B Correctional Facility for Boy's. WOW! The Board of Commissions was made up of wardens from different correctional facilities in Minnesota and other nearby states. I felt Mrs. Clog and others who was on the board was already against us kids. Because when Mrs. Clog sentenced me to Redwing for car theft I didn't even know how to drive! I started laughing at all of them sitting around the table. The people on the board was looking at me like I was crazy.

Wake up! My mind said, the fact was I didn't have nothing to say in my defense. I was just another black kid lost in a system that was not set up to rehabilitate me and succeed. This system was only meant to enslave me. Rehabilitation was not what this system was meant to do. According to what I've heard from other kids, both boys and girls; Lino Lakes had a barbed wire fence around the whole place. I imagined it to be like Duke Security Cottage in Red Wing. But when I arrived at Lino Lakes, I would find it was nothing like what I imagined.

So, here I go again! Back to being a caged animal going back to another barbed wire fence in the sky. Arriving at Lino Lakes was fascinating and scary at the same time. As we enter the grounds the large fence stood out. It surrounded the whole building, and the barbed wire covered the sky like a big umbrella covering a small town. This place seemed liked, not only did it want to strip a kid of their dignity, but it also wanted to infest your mind body and soul negatively. This place was cold, hollow, had no heart, had no soul, and saw young people as inhumane beings that could never change; and deserved no compassion or assistance to change.

I had a feeling this place was going to teach me more about becoming a better criminal than a productive member of society. While waiting to be checked in, I started day-dreaming once again. I was wondering what the gang I broke out of Red Wing with was doing? Were they living it up somewhere? Did they all get away! Did they know where I was? Were they thinking of a way to break me out of here? If I was still on the street, if the shoe was on the other foot I would be thinking what can we do to get our friend out of Lino.

When your locked up, you always have time to think about your past. Like one of my first girlfriend's I fell in love with came to mind. I left her out of my thoughts because of the shame I brought down on her family. Her family owned a big construction company and I remember shooting up the place. They were having a teen dance and her new boyfriend was dancing with her. Later that evening when we saw her dad go to work, the gang and I went to my ex-girlfriend's house.

We went in the house with guns. I made up my mind she was going to listen to what I had to say. Her sister came into the room. I told her sister to let her mom know we did not want any trouble. I just wanted to talk to her daughter, J for a little bit. Then me and the rest of the gang will leave and no one would be hurt. While Kenney was in kitchen looking around. We took the family's word that there was no one else in the house and that they would let me talk to my exgirlfriend without calling the police or anyone else.

I kept my promise about not hurting anyone. I let J. know how I felt about her writing me a dear john letter while I was in Red Wing. After saying what I wanted to say we left her house. I really loved J., as a kid would love a girl, she was scared of me. J. knew I was crazy. She knew I had done some thuggish things in my young life so far (armed robbery, drinking, and breaking out of a correctional facility). And her parents did not want her to have anything to do with me. I cannot say directly I would have shot her, but because of the frame of mind I was in, it was a strong possibility. I was hurt. I was angry. I thought I was in love and violence was the only way I knew to handle hurt and pain. I didn't care about my life, so how could I have cared about hers.

My life, her life, or anyone else's at that time meant nothing to me. J. knew I didn't want to shoot her. But I think she also knew I was hurt. I felt she saw the pain I was feeling, which made me even madder. Because if she knew my pain, she should not have sent me a dear john letter while I was locked up. Because you don't do that to people you care about. I was also mad at her for not trying to understand my feelings. All I wanted was to be loved and J. pushed me away.

I was surprised that her family did not call the police on us. But her sister did come out the door yelling at me and telling me how crazy I was, and she was glad her sister broke up with me. Geino looked at me and said, "Do you want me to turn around and just shoot her?" Geino was always ready to pull the trigger. I said, "No. Just keep walking." I was getting mad and was glad we left the house when we did.

The gang and I continued on our robbery spree, stealing from the rich (people we perceived to be rich) and giving to the poor. We was the poor! And we knew we was poor. Wake up! My daydream was interrupted by a guard yelling at us (the young people I was sent to Lino Lakes with). The guard told us to line up and to put on these outfits (prison attire). Then us new kids was put in what looked, like oversized dog cages. Which the guards called lockup cells.

The only good thing about checked in at Lino Lakes was seeing kids that I knew from being in other joints and hanging out in and the streets. After getting locked in our cells it was good to catch up on the news from the streets and what was going on, here at Lino Lakes. The in's and out's; and what to do and not what to do while you were here. The kids who were here told us to listen to the kids more than guards because the kids pretty much ran the joint. Even though the guards didn't think so.

Some of the guys had already heard I was on my way up the food chain. In other words, they knew I was on my way up to Lino Lakes. Big Blue (a guy I knew from the streets) greeted me with a head nod, as well as Richard and Scotty when they saw me. One thing I knew for sure was there would be no breaking out and running away from this place. The things I would see and experience here at Lino didn't make me scared but did make me smart. I saw how they wanted you to yell and scream so they (the guards) could beat you down. I saw how they (the guards) would put your food on a tray and dump some of it in the trash before it got to you.

I saw Richard get stripped all the way down to his shorts, his mattress taken out of his cell, while he his hands and ankles were handcuffed to his bed frame. They left him like that until morning. Then the guards would walk by with a cup of water and throw the water in Richard's face. From my cell I would see Richard's neck move. It seemed like he was trying to get as much of the water they threw at him down his throat. Then Richard would start yelling at the guards "Your not going to win! I hate you white so and so's! You're not going to break me!"

Then he would fight and struggle with his handcuffs that were chained to the bedframe. I felt the anger and rage creep up inside of me! I heard Big Blue and Scotty yelling for the guards to let Richard go. Even the white kids were yelling for the guards to let Richard go. I know those metal straps from the bed frame Richard was laying on were hurting him. I never even saw a dog get treated the way guards treated Richard. So, when you see another kid you know getting beat the way they beat him with hand cuffs on it just reminded me more and more how much I hated this system that seemed to let guards mistreat kids.

They left Richard that way until late that afternoon. Then they took him out of his cell, and I did not see my friend Richard again! He never returned to B-building. I hoped Richard was not dead, but I never did find out if was he was okay. Man it felt like months and months had passed by, but here I was back on the streets. My mom still lived over in south Minneapolis, MN where I started going to high school with my four other siblings. We were all back home. My three brothers and one sister had been in foster homes. My brother that was next in age to me was following in my footsteps and he also, ended up doing some time at Red Wing Correctional Facility.

It was good to see my family again. We had not seen each other in 4 years, since I left Detroit and moved back to Minneapolis. My mom had got married again and they both had good jobs. My mom was a nurse and my new stepdad was a male nurse. My new stepdad was cool. He drove a nice, brand new 1969 Lincoln Continental. We (my family and I were now living in a middle-class part of town. The neighborhood was quiet and clean, Once, my family arrived the question became, would the neighborhood stay that way? I guess the neighbors didn't know who we was. My cousins and family was coming to dinner like the Beverly Hillbillies, Uninvited and without the Truck! But in a Lincoln Continental. The south side of Minneapolis would never be the same!

THE HOUSE CALLED DYSFUNCTION!

I USE THE 1960's tv comedy show called *The Beverly Hillbillies*, to offer an explanation of how our family household was run. The TV series *The Beverly Hillbillies* started in 1962 and ran till 1971. The series was about a family who struck oil and became millionaires overnight. This luck of fortune gave them the money to move from the mountains to the city. And not just a city but what would be called an elite, exclusive city for those with the monetary means to afford a life-style most could only dream of.

However, once the hillbillies got to the city, they brought their personalities and way of thinking with them. They also brought their values with them and there lies the twist in the show. The country folk were trying to fit into city life and shape their values to a world that is not just foreign to them but relentlessly unforgiving by continuously showing them they are different.

They are not of this city life world nor familiar with the way things operate. Because the hillbillies were new money (money that was not part of family lineage) versus the city dwellers who either were from family lineage money or earned it. Family lineage money would be characterized as old money. An example of old money would be the Rockefeller's who owned Standard Oil Company. Rules that people make up to not only distinguish themselves from others they deem beneath them but also to exclude those they deem to be beneath them as well.

The tv show portrayed the hillbillies as being fools and dumb, but on the contrary. The hillbillies were far from being stupid. They just did things their own way. The hillbillies were unapologetic about doing things their own way but also tried to learn how their new city neighbors did things. Not to 'fit in' but to create harmony amongst their new neighbors and in their new surroundings.

My family played more outside the lines than the hillbillies. We moved into South Minneapolis and did not always understand the rules of our new neighbors and new community. But what we did understand was we were going to play by our rules. Our neighbors would either like it or call the police. Most of the time they called the police. And all the time we didn't care if they liked it.

Chaos, drama, mayhem and destruction were regular residents in our home. The residents of chaos, drama, mayhem, and destruction were not just visitors; they came in sat down and got very, comfortable. Calmness and peace rarely visited our household and quite honestly, I think we stirred up trouble when things did calm down because calmness and peace were not just seen as boring, but were viewed as unproductive in the monetary (money making) sense. However, the dysfunction the chaos created was as funny as it was serious. And when our relatives joined us funny became hilarious and chaos, mayhem, and destruction came with capital letters: CHAOS, MAYHEM, and DESTRUCTION!

Our relatives moved to Minnesota, from California, Detroit, Alabama, Kansas City, and Philadelphia the dysfunction was already comfortable and now it would be multiplied in our household and divided amongst the households of our relatives. The relatives who did not move into their own houses stayed with my family. Our house became full of aunts, uncles, and cousins. South Minneapolis never saw us coming and would never be the same once we settled in, took-a-look around, and saw what we could get into.

My family was not rich, but we were not poor either. Even with my mom and stepdad working there was still a lot of parties, drug abuse, fights, drinking, and other types of negative behaviors. Our house was the dope house and the party house. Our house stood out in the prominent South Minneapolis neighborhood. Like Santa Claus standing in the middle of the street in the middle of July during a Las Vegas summer.

When the police showed up at our house, which seemed like every other day, Everyone at home played stupid, as if they didn't know why police were being called to the house. Even though neighbors, family, and friends in and at our house could see new Lincoln and Cadillac cars parked all the way down the block. Oftentimes the cars owners would be sitting on our porch to greet the cops to stop them from walking into our house, uninvited if they needed to.

Kids at our house could pretty much do what they wanted to do because there was no discipline in our house unless you got caught doing something wrong. And wrong was often defined by the person who caught you. Even if what you did was considered wrong, your punishment was usually going to be getting your butt whipped with a belt. Whippings with a belt for most of us kids was just a faster way to deal with your punishment so you could go back to what you were doing before you got whipped.

I remember when people partying at our house would fall asleep in the living room; my brother and I would take wooden stick matches and put them in between the sleeper's toes or in their sock. We would then watch the sleeper from under the dining table. As he or she would jump up and look around while shaking their legs and kicking their foot, another person who would be sleep near the person shaking their legs and kicking their foot would get kicked.

And then a fight would break out and the person who's foot was burning from the match and the person who got kicked by the person who was trying to put out the match never knew how the fight began. But the fight would give me and my brother time to crawl from under the dining room table, run back to our bedroom, and laugh so hard our sides would hurt.

The next day I would hear my cousin yelling in the front yard that someone tried to burn his girlfriend's toes up. I would again laugh until my side hurt. One cousin was yelling at another cousin about the toe fire incident. The other cousin yelled back, "Her feet was smelling so bad they caught on fire?!" Thinking about that argument today still makes me laugh.

My cousins was having this argument while barbecuing out in front yard. I was watching and thought there was going to be a barbecue rib fight. Because the argument had gotten rather heated for a minute. But they went back to smoking their weed and drinking their beer. Front yard barbecuing became a regular event as other friends and family members started gathering at our house.

Friends and family members would bring barrels and trash cans filled with ice, all kinds of beer, wine, and liquor. As a kid I thought my family gathered out in the front yard because back in the 30's, 40's, 50's, and even the 60's blacks were not allowed to come into the front doors of business establishments and white people's homes. They (black people) could only use the back door and gather in the kitchen or the back yard. That was not the case at my family's house.

My uncles and cousins was selling dope and stolen goods out back in our garage. The stolen goods were mostly guns. So, I think to keep people's attention away from the backyard was the other reason why my family barbecued and hung out in the front yard. The backyard was for business. Barbecuing in the front yard also meant people was paying more attention to what was going on in the front of our house.

School was just as interesting for us as home. My sister got kicked out of school for stabbing a girl in her class. She told my mom she was angry before she left the house because someone drank her pop (soda pop) that was in the ice box. My mom did not whup my sister she put her on punishment but also bought her some chicken and another pop to make up for someone drinking hers.

Reverend Roy's mom

My brothers were either playing hooky or running around with their own crowds. Speaking for myself I liked high school because I was learning how to be an entrepreneur. I was showing my new clique of school friends about the winery business. In other words, I was selling liquor in the back of our high school parking lot at lunch time. I had all types of wines, from Ariba, Spanada, Balley's, Ripple, and yes; I had even Thunderbird. You could mix the Thunderbird with Kool-Aid and would have your own cocktail.

The school kids loved my cocktail. The good thing was, that it would only cost you an extra quarter if I had to shake the wine and Kool-Aid up for you. I had to figure out ways to charge extra because help didn't come cheap. I had to pay my cousin Earnest who lived with us to get the liquor for me. By my standards, my life was going fine, in1969, I hooked up with Kenney who looked me up when he got out of the joint. He heard I was staying in South Minneapolis. They (Department of Corrections) had sent him back to Red Wing. When Kenney came to see me, he was with another kid named Sam-Sam. He lived in North Minneapolis. Sam-Sam had never been to the joint, but Kenney said Sam-Sam had heart. Kenney said he met Sam-Sam through Walter while he was staying in Walter's basement in the northside Minneapolis housing projects.

Kenney told me the night we all split up after the grocery store robbery; Robert, Walter, and him stayed together with Geino. They never did split up. They said they heard I got caught when they ran into C.C. at Old Henry's (the hamburger joint). My grandfather told her I got caught. Kenney also told me they had nowhere to stay because I was not with them.

Then Kenney got this sad look on his face. Kenney said. "Lee, Geino tried to jack (steal) a car for us. It was an undercover cop. The cop shot Geino! He's dead! When Geino told him (the undercover cop) to hand over his wallet, the cop emptied his gun into Geino. Kenney then told me that Robert, Walter, and him took off running. But before they ran, they saw the whole thing. I said, "Wow!! Geino had to be close to 16 years old because he was a year younger than me. And I had just turned 17.

Wow!! I said again. Even though we was involved in behavior that could mean we would or could be shot it was still startling to hear a cop shot a 15 or 16 year-old kid. I really liked Geino. He was the only Italian kid that I knew who had heart, like we did. Robert got ahold of his aunt who lived up in Detroit Lakes Minnesota and went to live with her.

Kenney said he got caught at Walter's house when Walter's dad called the police on Walter, for stealing a pair of his dad's socks. Kenney said, "Walter's dad also made Walter take the socks off before the police took us away." The last Kenney heard anything about Walter he was going to get his mother's permission to join the Marines. I told Kenney he and Sam-Sam can stay at our place. Our 5 bedrooms; two-bathroom house was already full, two more occupants wasn't going to hurt.

Two friends staying at my house eventually became four. Tommy and J.C. were two black kids who lived down by 35th street and Chicago Avenue in south Minneapolis. They started hanging out with us, along with C.W. and Richie. C.W. and Richie had already done time at Glen Lake Boys Home. Our gang quickly went from 3 people to 9 people. Bobby and Grover joined us a few weeks later. They also lived on the south side of Minneapolis.

Now, teens close to being young adults we was getting into all kinds of trouble. I was barely attending school. In fact, I was only going to school to check on my entrepreneur business (selling alcohol at lunch time). In my mind I was doing the high school a service by giving the students something to look forward to at lunch time. Because the students were coming to school to buy my drugs: speed, acid, weed, hash and alcohol. I liked to think they were coming to school for higher learning that only alcohol and drugs could provide; brain stimulation to inspire an educational mind set and nutritional encouragement (as weed/marijuana) gives people the munchies. I would think to myself no need to thank me, being an entrepreneur has its own rewards.

Even though the school principal and teachers couldn't prove I was dealing drugs and selling alcohol to students they still wanted me to transfer to a different school, Central High School. Central was on 35th & 4th Avenue South. The teachers at the school I was currently attending gave me passing grades and sent me on my way, to Central. I think they were scared, of me and my gang. Which also gave them another reason to kick me out.

Now that I had time off from school and my business (taking time off from selling drugs and alcohol), at the age of almost 17 our house became even more popular, crazy, and dangerous. Our house became the dope, stolen goods, and prostitution factory. All this going on while my friends and friends of my brothers and sister lived with us. My brothers and sister grew up fast. The fast lane was trying to keep up with them. We were all behaving like the adults that were around us: drinking, smoking, using drugs, and having sex. So, things like assaults, drug overdoses, drug abuse, and suicide attempts, were normal to our family. I don't think we viewed our behaviors as wrong. I think we viewed our behaviors as; survival and get them before they get you.

Everyone in our house was doing their own thing. And I was no different. I was undisciplined and running wild! I was experimenting with all kinds of drugs: speed, acid, purple haze, orange sunshine, and hash. Liquor started becoming my best friend. Kenney was my first bestfriend but alcohol was a very, close second. Kenney was second in command of our gang as well. Kenney was second in command because I knew him. And I knew I could trust him to have my back under any circumstance. Kenney and I was boys for life!

Reflecting for a moment Dr. Greg Thomas asked, "Can you break the cycle of generational dysfunction?" He writes, "Often some of our deepest personal problems are rooted in something we can't control.

Dysfunctional family behavioral patterns that came before us. But we can control our choices, and each of us choose life and good things."

I beg to differ! What if you are a kid, and you are caught up in a culture of dysfunction? And a world, that is overly infested with abnormal norms layered with evasive action because of the color of your skin?! In this setting, good cannot only become skewed it can become rare. There is so much injustice surrounding skin color that locking a kid away and taking them away from their family was/is called rehabilitation, but in actuality is/does create a place for unusual punishment that only exacerbates the negative feelings of a young person that came from already crippling circumstances.

Being sent back up north to Minneapolis from Detroit I really didn't see it (this vicious cycle of ill treatment) or feel something was wrong till I was in the Plymouth Avenue Riots over in North Minneapolis. I was locked up in the system, I was already in a dysfunctional spiral, I was so busy being bad that it seemed like the only time I would think about God and good, is when I would think about my grandmother. I had an understanding, of good but good was not displayed in my home regularly.

I understood God existed but only knew Him as someone my grandmother prayed to. Today when I look back, I believe even though God was not in my program, I was in His. Me and my little gang was doing a lot of running for the family (my family). Meaning we were selling a lot of stolen guns, drugs, dress clothes, and sometimes candy to cover up (camouflage) the drugs.

We did this for my uncle and cousins that brought back merchandise from Chicago and Detroit. We would go up and down 4th Avenue, Park Avenue, and Lake Street to Clinton Avenue, back down 5th Avenue, and 3rd Avenue, to the gambling houses, after hour joints, and bootleg joints selling the stuff.

The gang's cut meant my family kept us supplied with liquor, drugs alcohol and money. My crew and I had a good thing going.

Sometimes we would get dressed and go down to the Nacirema on 40th and 4th Avenue South. The bouncers would let us little thugs in because they were our customers or my family's customers. Things were going well until kids in the gang started getting greedy. The more money we made, the more alcohol, drugs, and money we wanted.

While hanging out at the Spruce Lounge that was on 4th Avenue and 38th Street, some of our gang often liked to hang around in the back of the lounge where some of the prostitutes and tricks were at. We liked to hang out back because the prostitutes thought we were cute. They knew we were young but that didn't matter to us. The important thing was they thought we was cute. We thought we were doing something with our big talk and acting older than we were.

On this night, one of our associates Bobby came up to us and reported to us that a person at one of the bootleg houses needed some guns right away and they was willing to pay almost double for them. Bobby was still kind of new in our gang. He had only been around us for a few months. But he was cool. I told him I would get back to him in a few hours. I made that decision because there was no need to rush since it was still early in the evening. Kenney and J.C. was standing by as me and Bobby was having the conversation about the guns. I told J.C. to go inside and get Tommy and Sam-Sam so we could go to my house and do the deal with my family. When we got there my cousin was not there. But I knew where my stepdad kept some of his guns. At that time, I didn't know he was in the racket with my uncles and cousins.

I took four of his pistols, two 22s and two 38s. Sam-Sam sat in the car that Tommy was driving. A brown 1967 Buick Deuce and a Quarter. Tommy honked the horn for Kenney, J.C. and I to hurry on up. As soon as we got in the car Tommy skidded away from the curb. A few minutes later we ended up at the Johnny Baker Post on 5th Avenue and Lake Street. The spot where we was to meet Bobby and the gun buyer.

The transaction went well. We even made more money selling a 1/4 pound of weed (marijuana) we had on us. I wanted to get back to house so I could let the family and my stepdad know we made him an extra profit. We got back to house. Tommy parked in the back of the house where our driveway was located. We was all going to go back down to the Nacirema after I took care of business in the house.

Kenney was behind me while everyone else stayed in the car. I put my key into the door and we went from kitchen to the dining room. My brother Ricky was waving his hands like he was trying to tell me to go back or something. But it was too late! I saw two of my cousins take Kenney at gun point with a pistol to his head.

The next thing I knew my head was met with the butt of a shot gun! I felt like I was being hit with a hot steel pipe! As I was getting whipped with a shot gun, I felt like I was going to die, or needed to! I felt as though I was not coming out the house alive! I felt like I was being dragged somewhere. Why is it so dark? I can't hear anything but muffled sounds. I slipped into darkness.

> Therefore whatever you have said in the dark shall be heard in the light, and what you have whispered in private rooms shall be proclaimed on the housetops.
>
> —Luke 12:3
> English Standard Version (ESV)

The voice in my head once again telling me to Wake up! I heard doctors' names being called. With one eye open I could see a nurse pull back a curtain. She smiled as she asked me how I was feeling? I spoke to her in what seemed like a whisper. My throat was dry, my head was pounding, my arms and legs felt real sore, and I felt like I could only hear out of one ear.

I said, "Where am I?" The nurse answered, "In General Hospital in Downtown Minneapolis by the National Guard Armory." As she was lifting my body up to give me some water, she said my friends was sitting outside. I asked her if she could call my friends in while she went to get the doctor. She smiled with a little wink and said, she would see what she could do.

When Kenney, Sam-Sam, Bobby, J.C., Tommy, and C.W. came into the room they acted like I just won the football game for the team. Kenney said, "Man! Oh Man! I thought we both was dead! They had me watch you get beat up. Then they took all my money and my gun, and the money you had Lee. I tried to explain to one of your uncles that we was just trying to make your stepdad knew he had made a profit.

They (my uncles and cousins) told me the guns were not my step-dads they belong to the family. They said, "The only reason why you (Kenney) was living is because they wanted me to give you the message!" They said, "They would drop your things and any of our things off at another one of your cousin's houses, but we are not to stay there (at your mom's house anymore). You don't steal from family." Kenney then told me, my family had him drag me to the car and told the rest of my gang at gun point that we was on our own. That we are not to do anymore running for them or pick up any more money. Yes, my uncles and cousins were teaching me and my crew to stay in our place (mind our business).

We all knew we was all lucky to be living. My family told my crew to take me to the hospital and say I was robbed. It was a good thing Kenney told me what happened. Because the doctor walked in with the nurse and my mother just as Kenney had finished telling me what I was supposed to say. The nurse told all the guys they would have to leave the room.

The doctor asked me what happened. I said, "Doc I was walking down Park Avenue and 36th when two white guys jumped me. The only reason I said two white guys was because they would let the case go. If I would of said two black guys, there might have been more questioning by the doctor, police, a line up or pictures to look at.

I thought that's why my mom was there. But the family told her where I was. They told my mom they wasn't trying to kill me. They was just trying to teach me a lesson. My mom knew I couldn't stay back with my grandmother, 'cause I had went from bad to worse with my behavior. I knew my mom loved me, she just wanted me to be safe. So, she told me to stay away from our house. The doctor told me I had no broken bones. But I did have a fractured ear drum. All and all I was ok and could go home. What home, I thought to myself.

Again, God and his angel's must have been around me without me even knowing it. What I mean is, I don't remember even calling out God's name or asking God for his help! I didn't believe God helped us bad kids, once again. As we left the hospital the gang was glad to see my mom. They had a lot of respect for my mom. The guys thought my mom was fun because my mom would be keeping up with the teen dances just like us.

My mom had told me she called a friend of hers named Anna, who lived over north. I knew the whole family. Anna and her husband Buster was just like a second mom and dad to me. I became their foster child along with some of my other brothers and sister. Anna's son Jimmy who was about 19 years old was looking for an apartment. So, while I was staying with Jimmy's family, my mom and his mom agreed to help us out (pay bills, buy groceries) if we found a place. I was glad to be back at Anna and Buster's home. It put me back in North Minneapolis. Although, l still had my South Minneapolis gang.

Jimmy was not part of our gang, but he was cool. He did a few robberies with us. Breaking into jewelry stores and stealing cars. Jimmy and I found an apartment over in South Minneapolis. We got along ok. He would look the other way when it came to the criminal activities I was doing. And I would look away from his drug habit. Our apartment turned into a club house. And still attending Minneapolis Central High School I had a different clientele for the drug business I started at my previous high school.

The kids at Central was getting off more on heroin, speed, and sleeping pills. Now everybody wanted to deal at Central. This meant there was a lot more competition from other drug dealers and gangs for customers at the school. Knowing the competition for customers had increased my crew decided to pull out of that game and went back to strong armed robbery. Me and Jimmy's apartment turned into a hangout for dealers, parties, girls, and sex. I was hardly going to school. I was just getting high and having fun.

One day while driving down 4th Avenue me and some guys was passing by some girls wearing school uniforms. They were on their way to one of the catholic high schools over in South Minneapolis. There was one girl that stood out in the crowd. She was tall, skinny, brown-skinned and looked like a plain Jane by my standards. But there was something about her that made her seem so innocent.

From the world I was living in that quality was attractive to me. It took me a few weeks, but I kept having my crew or sometimes Jimmy take me down the same streets where I first saw her. I would see three or four of her friends walking to school. But not her. Kenney and J.C. would be laughing at me. I thought what did I see in this square girl who wouldn't even give me her name?

Kenney said let's get back to your pad (apartment) Lee where we got some real hot girls who are skipping school from Central High coming over at lunch time. I laughed right along with them and said, "Yeah, you're right Kenney." But in my mind, I had other plans. It was time I learned to drive. Jimmy started taking me over to North Minneapolis to Market Square, which was located across the street from the Munsingwear Warehouse. We would then go from Lyndale and Glenwood, onto the freeway. I was going 85 miles an hour. I learned how to drive really quick. I was quite pleased with myself.

Learning to drive meant, I was now in that part of my life where I was moving and living in the fast lane! Now I need a car. I took some of my money and went to see a man I knew who ran a gambling joint behind Kurt Gas Station over in South Minneapolis. He was selling a few cars and it didn't matter if you had a license. Your money was license enough. I had enough money to pull out of his backyard with a 1966 Ninety-Eight Oldsmobile. It was black with fake gangster white wall tires. I knew the tires were fake white walls because the white on the tire was glued. The tire factory paints white on the tire that does not peel away. However, the paint does get scratched if the driver gets too close to the curb.

Tommy, Sam-Sam, Kenney, J.C., and Bobby was the first to ride in my new car. Jimmy declined to get in. He thought it might be stolen. I felt like I was on top of the world. I had an apartment, a cool roommate, a good crew that kept the money rolling in, and I was even getting back in good standing with my family. Everything was ok.

RAILROADED WITH TRACKS OF MAKE BELIEVE DEALS

Be kind to one another, tenderhearted, forgiving one another, as God in Christ forgave you.

—Ephesians 4:32
English Standard Version (ESV)

As KENNEY, JC and I thought we was on our way downtown to the juvenile center. the police ended up driving down 3rd street in downtown Minneapolis to the clock, otherwise known as the court-house, which housed the Minneapolis jail. The courthouse was made of brown brick that looked like a castle with a big clock at the top of the tower. I heard people talk about it (the jail under the clock), when you went up under the clock and stayed more than a day, you was in jail waiting for bail. That courthouse with the clock still stands today in downtown Minneapolis. Back to the backseat of the police car, me and Kenney started talking 'cause I wanted to know what happened at my apartment.

72

But the police told us to shut our mouth if we wanted to make it to our destination in one piece. Or they would make a u-turn and we could wind up somewhere else. I wanted to ask why we was at the clock instead of the juvenile center. But I kept my mouth shut. Once we arrived at the clock, the three of us was put in a holding cell with some other guys. The jailer said that a detective would be talking to us just as soon as our parents came down to the courthouse. When the jailer left I asked Kenney and JC what happened back at the apartment.

Kenney started talking. I could tell JC was high, which was not unusual for JC, that joker stayed high. But still, he was quiet, which made me wonder with everything Kenney is sharing about what happened why JC don't have nothin' to say? Kenney said after I left the house earlier that day, him Jimmy, Tommy, and C.W. went to go get something to eat. They met three girls and another cat (guy) up by the high school near the apartment. They all went back to the apartment and started getting high. And the party was on. Jimmy took one of the girls into the bedroom and started having sex with her. Other guys that were in the apartment came into the bedroom as well.

They began to pull a train (several people having sex with someone), on the girl Jimmy had brought to the bedroom. Kenney said JC was one of them. JC spoke up for the first time. He said, "The girl wanted to have sex with everyone in the house." It might have been the pills Jimmy gave her. "But it's my apartment!" JC said in a loud voice. But its Jimmy's apartment too, right? Kenney could see I was getting mad! I said JC, "You don't take no orders from Jimmy or no chick! You take orders from me and Kenney!" I then turn my eyes back on Kenney who continued to tell me what happened.

We was all having fun. The other two girls was dancing with us and having a good time. Then this cat who came with the girls started wanting some dope on the house (for free or to pay later). He wanted some free dope 'cause he seen me giving more dope to the young ladies. Kenney said, "And after I told the guy you're not dancing like the ladies.

He got mad." He told the girls he was ready to go right now." He said that because he brought them to the apartment. The girls laughed at the guy. And told him they was not going anywhere. And they was going to wait on their girlfriend that was in the bedroom with the other guys.

After hearing that the guy left. About an hour later we heard a knock at the door. It was the guy. I thought he came back with some more money. He came back with police! So, the guy must of been one of the undercover snitches for the police department. Because the girls said they didn't know him that well either. They just seen him hanging out at the school a lot. Kenney said, "The next thing I know Lee, the police had their guns out. And one of the police said you little nappy-headed @*&%# make my day! Kenney said the gang didn't have time to pick up the guns they was carrying. Or get rid of any of the dope. The guys in the bedroom got caught with their paints down!" Kenney said to me, You know the rest."

I said, Wow Kenney! The money we was saving! Our dope! Our guns all gone!" JC said, "Sorry man. But maybe they would give us the money back if we tell the police we earned it by working!" Me and Kenney looked at JC and thought not only was this boy high, he's stupid! Even though JC was black, we knew he'd been hanging with white folk for too long! JC knew none of us even knew what a social security card looked like. We didn't know how to apply for a social security card and we had no interest in 9 to 5 labor. We all sat in jail laughing so hard the jailer had to tell us to quiet down.

I was wondering what Jimmy and the rest of our gang was doing. They had to also be here under the clock as well. As the three of us started getting tired Kenney suggested that one of us stay awake. We thought we should be alert because there was a few older guys in the cell we didn't know. We found a spot in one of the corners of the cell that had a cold steel bench. While Kenney was telling me what happened, the three of us had been standing up in the cell the whole time. While we were talking, we forgot we were in a cell and needed to secure a spot to sleep.

I also thought about our gang was cut in size by more than half. We didn't know where the police had taken the rest of our gang. We didn't know how long it would be before we got to see them again. And we didn't know how this adult jail cell thing worked. Adult jail was new territory to us. We let JC go to sleep first, seeing he was high anyway. He wouldn't have been any help if something had popped off in this jail cell. I fell off into a deep sleep as well. I was awakened by the jailer slamming the steel doors. Kenney was still awake and off into his own thoughts. Since the jailer woke me up with the slamming of cell doors, I told Kenney to get some sleep. We let JC keep on snoring.

JC got so loud at times, we thought other guys in the cell was going to say something.

But they didn't. I guess they was thinking about their cases too. I don't know what time it was but it had to be early in the morning, 'cause I heard the clanking of trays. I also saw little cartons of milk and breakfast rolls on the trays. The jailers was handing each of us a roll and a milk. JC must of smelled the food 'cause he woke right up from his sleep. "Wow!" I said out loud. "What happened to supper! What time is it? And don't I get a phone call?!" The jailer looked at me like I was from another planet. He then said in a very loud voice, "When your done with the delicious breakfast the state has provided you, put your wrappers and cartons into the trash that will be coming around." Then the jailer walked away.

One of the older guys said, "Don't pay any attention to him young blood (young man), it's about 6:30 a.m. You're a juvenile, so the police makes your phone call. And you missed dinner. Which consisted of bologna and cheese on 2 slices of white bread with no mayo. And its brought in at 5 p.m. way before you little cats got here." I nodded my head in thanks and went back to eating my roll. Kenney was waking up now. JC was looking at Kenney's milk and roll that I had dropped in Kenny's lap. I said to JC with a facial expression on my face that let him know if he ate Kenney's roll I was going to whup his a#%, I told JC, "If you touch Kenney's roll I am going to bite into you the way you want to bite into Kenney's roll."

After I said that I gave a couple of growls! JC got a little nervous. Everyone in the cell started laughing, including JC. JC was laughing, but he knows at a party the gang and I was at a while back I bit a piece off of someone's face off and spit it out my mouth. JC knew how mad and angry I could get. Kenny was still laughing as the both of us tossed a part of our roll to JC at the same time. While we're sitting there finishing our rolls I heard keys jangling as the cell door started to open. The jailer called my name. The jailer took me to another part of the building where I was led into a small room with a mirror that looked like a window. There was a wooden table with chairs and the lights above the ceiling was shining so bright that I had to cover my eyes for a moment.

The jailer left the handcuffs on me and sat me down in one of the chairs. He left out of the room, it seemed like I was sitting in the small room for a very, long time. When the door finally opened, I saw my mom with two big police detectives behind her. She came toward me to give me a hug. As I was quickly getting up from the chair to greet my mom, one of the detectives put his hand on my shoulder. He was pushing down on my shoulder to push me back down in the chair, while ordering me to sit back down. The other detective stood in between my mom and me. He told her we could not touch each other. I thought, Oh boy! Was I being treated like criminal with a capitol C.

The detective started right in on me. Telling me I had multiple charges which ranged from having guns and drugs to having girls have sex for money in my apartment. The detective also said, I had guys in the apartment who had gang ties. Now I'm getting mad! Because I was not a pimp! And speaking of money nothing was mentioned about the grands (money) that was taken out of me and Kenney's safe. So, these detectives are liars and thieves is what I'm thinkin'.

Even though I knew the story from Kenney and JC because they told me when we were in the jail cell, I told the detective I didn't know anything. I told the detective I was not there. I also asked the detective, "Why did the police plant keys to a safe on me?" I knew I was lying on the police. But they were lying on me too. When I look back on this now, I think to myself as a kid I really had some nerve trying to justify my actions. But at the time, I figured they lied on me about me being there at the apartment, so why not lie on them. Plus, I was mad! The police took our hard earned money that we had worked for. Yes, during the time I was fully involved in street life, work was one of the ways I defined what I did.

My mom spoke up and said I should not say anything more without speaking to a lawyer or someone in my defense. The detectives agreed. As of right now I was looking at going back to Lino Lakes, the juvenile facility I had been in before, until I was 21. So, I did what my mom told me to do. I stopped talking to the detectives. Once the detectives knew I was not going to say anything else one of them helped me up from my chair and escorted my mom and I out into the hallway. They let my mom visit with me while they was getting paper work together before taking me back to my cell.

My mom told me that our house got raided while she was at work. She said some of my uncles, cousins and other people got busted as well. She continued to tell me that social services was going to be taking my sister and brothers out of our house and putting them in foster homes due to what social services called living in a dangerous household. I felt bad for my mom. I could see the tears behind her eyes as she said to me, "Lee, don't worry. I will get you a lawyer no matter what. We will fight this." I had shared with my mom that I was with a catholic girl I met named Destiny. She attended the all-girls catholic school in south Minneapolis. I told my mom the catholic school-girl and I were having lunch at the donut shop during the time the police claim I was at the apartment.

I also told my mom I needed her to get a hold of the girl and her parents 'cause she was my alibi. And I asked my mom to get in touch with a friend of mine, San that I was with for a while that day at the youth center on 48th avenue. My mom said she would see what she could do. I asked my mom about Jimmy, Kenney and the rest of the guys. She said she talked to Jimmy's mom and his mom said he was facing adult time. My mom said that's all she knew, right now. The jailer was coming back to take me to my cell. My mom and I said our goodbyes. I told her I loved her and she told me she loved me. My mother was there for me more then I knew.

A thought came across my mind that my grandmother use to tell me. If God is for me, who can be against me. I said to myself, "Man I have done a lot of things for God to be against me. And I haven't done anything for God to be for me. I'm thinking, I don't even have the right to ask God to help me out of this situation. And in my heart I knew I would not be going home any time soon. The jailer returned me back to the cell where Kenney an JC was at. Kenney and JC said their relatives had also came down to the courthouse to see them.

Kenney said they ran into Tommy in the courthouse hallway. Tommy told them he heard Jimmy was telling people he rented the apartment with me. I was trying to make a deal with the detectives and put the whole blame on us, cause we were juveniles. More specifically, me. After hearing that from Tommy I told Kenney, "Don't worry about Jimmy. That snitch! We'll deal with him later." Kenney and I knew that one of the rules of the game was, even if you knew something you didn't say anything. Once you say something you've broken the rules by snitching!

What made it even worse was Jimmy was not even one of us! He wasn't in our gang! I don't think he even knew how to spell the word! I told Kenney my mom was getting me a lawyer. I told Kenney we was going to stick to our story about the safe keys being put in our pocket by the police. And just flip the script on Jimmy with his snitching a%#. I told Kenney we'll say that it was his (Jimmy's) safe. And he's the one doing the gun running and drug selling. That way Kenney would only have to account for the gun and dope that was on his person.

JC would tell the same story. So, he would only have to account for the gun and drugs that he had on him as well.

All of our guy talk was interrupted by clinking and clacking of keys. The jailers were bringing lunch down the cell hallway. While lunch was coming down the hallway Kenney, JC and I could hear our names being called over the jail speaker above the noise and racket in the other cells. A jailer said, "You youngsters grab your delicious sandwich to go. You're on your way to going home, aka, back to the juvenile center. The jailer announced it so loudly the older guys in the cell started laughing. But they also gave us our respect as one of them said, "You young bloods stick to a plan. And remember you are the new black man!" Me and Kenney didn't know what the heck he was talking about. But we nodded like we understood.

Man, this might sound crazy but it, kind of felt good going back to the juvenile center. The juvenile center stay would be short lived. I wasn't even there for a week when they already had me set up for a hearing. Kenney was already set up for a hearing as well. JC did not make the court list we was on. I saw a few of the northsiders (people from the northside of Minneapolis) that was locked up on the same side I was while in jail. Once I was back at juvy (the juvenile center) boy, did it feel good to get a full hot meal instead of the stuff they gave you in adult detention, under the clock.

In juvy, the boys and girls eat in the same dining area. So, we got a little time to socialize with each other before getting locked up in our cell for the rest of the day. Sometimes the juvenile detention staff would have some kind of activity you could participate in for an hour or two. Then it would be dim the lights in the cell, time. Lights in juvy stayed on all night. I'm sure it was for everyone's safety. There was no way juvenile detention staff was going to turn the lights off in this place. At the time I didn't pay attention but I'm sure activities for juveniles in juvy was some half-hearted attempt to help the young people in the juvenile center. Maybe it was the juvenile staff's attempt to provide kids in juvy some sense normal young people stuff.

It felt good to finally stretch out in a bed. No matter where it was. But my mind was swimming and racing around thinking back to all of the events that is happening and that has happened in my 17 years of life. This could not be all there is to life. This could be all there was? The robbing, the gang banging, the drug dealing, hurting people, people hurting me; was this my destiny? Speaking of destiny; I just thought about the catholic girl Destiny I met. I really liked her, but now with this new case... I wondered if I would ever see her again.

I had all kinds of thoughts rambling around in my head. I just remembered one of the detectives from earlier saying to me that I only met with my probation officer (P.O.) one time when I was released from Lino Lakes. I truly thought when I got out was the only time that I was supposed to meet him. And I played dumb with the detective and gave the detective a smart mouth kid answer, "I thought the p in P.O. meant for me to give the probation officer the peace sign and the, o was for I am outta here.

I thought about my brothers and sister and wished I had been home to protect them from the raid at my mom's house and the social workers who came to put my brothers and sister in a foster home. Me and my gang would have robbed the social workers at gun point and put them (the social workers) in foster homes. I thought about my uncles, aunts, cousins, friends and the gang I admired back in Detroit. I thought about the picnics my family would have in Highland Park.

Boy! Minnesota sucks about right now! I remember watching a western on TV. It was about the outlaw, Jessie James and the James Gang. One of his gang members said, "Out of all the banks the gang robbed if they would not have robbed the bank in Northfield, Minnesota they would not have been caught. I kind of smiled and thought to myself, maybe God! was trying to tell us bad kids, if you do a crime, you will get caught. Especially in Minnesota. I knew I was tired because the rambling thoughts in my head were going silent. I fell into a deep sleep "WAKE UP! It's breakfast time." I heard a staff person say as they went around the detention center circle hallway, unlocking the cell doors for the kids to come out of their cell and eat. For some reason I felt more rested then, I did in a long time. Was it because I thought about, God for a moment? I sat at the folding table with Kenney and some guys and girls I knew from the northside of Minneapolis. Kenney also knew the guys as well from being in the joint. JC did not come down for breakfast. Maybe he was coming down from his high. If that boy didn't get high, which meant he was giving me money for his drugs, he would be useless.

It felt good chatting and laughing with others our age. Just as I was having fun Kenney's name and my name came across the loud-speaker. The voice from the loud-speaker said, we had to be ready for a hearing in family court in 45 minutes. The staff got both of us up from the table and took Kenney and I back to our cells. I thought to myself, now what?! The staff unlocked my cell door after what seemed like hours. Then I saw Kenney. Another juvenile detention staff person was waiting for us on the other side of the circle hallway. We both was escorted to the other side of the Hennepin County juvenile center building.

There was a bunch of folks standing out in the courtroom hallway waiting for their turn to go inside. As we were waiting a lady called Kenney's name and they went into the courtroom. As Kenney was escorted into a courtroom and I was sitting in the hallway outside the courtroom I looked up from the floor I was staring at and saw my mom. A tall white man was coming towards me. The juvenile detention staff that was with me didn't say anything. They didn't even try to stop me as I ran up and hugged my mom.

I suddenly felt like an innocent child again being held in my mother's arms. I was so happy to see her I didn't want to let go. I was clinging to her so tight I didn't even feel the tears that was running down my face. Once our embrace loosened my mom introduced me to the tall man. His name was Mr. Note. The juvenile detention staff that was with me lead the three of us to a small meeting room with three chairs and a steel table that didn't move. Mr. Note started talking first. He told me that he was the lawyer my mom hired. He said he had already started investigating my case. Mr. Note said from what my mom had told him all they would have to do is get witness statements saying I was not there (at the apartment) while, and if; a crime was or had taken place. If those providing statements say I had nothing to do with what was going on in the apartment, then I could go home.

Wow! I thought to myself this lawyer is good. But, the lawyer said, looking at my mom and me with concerned eyes; the police said in the car you had parked outside your apartment they found a gun and some pills. And you don't have registration or license to operate a motor vehicle. So, they are checking to see if the car is stolen. "I can argue all that!" Said the lawyer. "Because you were not in the car at the time of your arrest. But, the only way I can accomplish that, is if they certify you as an adult. Right now, the prosecutors want the judge to keep you locked up until your passed 21 because of your past record. They don't need new charges to keep you here. But, the lawyer said. Now I was getting upset. I was also getting tired of these @%$&^* buts.

I said to myself if I hear one more BUT from this lawyer I am going to pick up this table that don't move up and throw it at him. The lawyer said again, "If you let me talk to the judge about putting you in the adult court system you can be home in a week, two weeks at the most." I saw my mom nod her head for me to say yes to what the lawyer was offering. And yes it was. I wanted to go home. We left the meeting room to go into court. Once in court the bailiff called my name. I stood up in front of the judge. The lawyer was right, the attorney for the state wanted me held over for adult court right away.

As Kenney and I left the court room Kenney said the prosecutors was talking about his case being turned over to adult court 'cause his birthday was coming up in a few weeks. But the judge did not decide at that time if Kenney's case would be sent to adult court. I told Kenney my past stuff (juvenile record) was so bad the judge wanted to hurry up and get rid of me. We both started laughing. I told Kenney I would be out in a week or two so I would come to visit him and make sure the money was on his books. I thought to myself Kenney might have to do some serious time because of the weapon and drug charges.

We was both in a good mood as we went back to our cells. Both Kenney and I was concerned about JC. We had not seen or heard from him and it was lunch time. JC was not in the dining area when all us kids was let out of our cells. I asked one of the staff if he could check to see what happened to our friend JC. I thought maybe he was still just too tired to come out of his cell and socialize with the rest of us. The staff person said he would look into it.

Even though we were being locked back in our rooms I still felt pretty, good! I wish I could have said goodbye to my mom. I also wish she had not seen me cry like some baby. But they took us out of the court room through a door that was different from the door we used to enter the courtroom. The staff person kept his word. He told me and Kenney that our friend JC was at General Hospital in downtown Minneapolis. General Hospital was not too far from the juvenile center we were at But that was all he could tell us.

I was really concerned now. Because JC didn't look or seem sick to us. I said to Kenney, "Something just isn't right. JC, high, yes. JC, sick no. I hope he is ok." Kenney laughed and said, "You know how JC is. He is probably playing sick so he can get some more drugs." I smiled and said, "You are so right Kenney I forgot how smooth JC was with game." JC was cool and slick like the rest of us. He could well, hold his own. It seemed like months instead of a week. before my lawyer got back to me. Mr. Note said I would being going to court soon, and he had everything he needed. He got statements from Destiny (the catholic schoolgirl), the donut shop waitress, and my friend San. Mr. Note also said the car did not come back stolen! But they (prosecutors) wanted to know where I got the car from?

I lied and told Mr. Note I won the car from a kid in a dice game. I said the guy told me he was going to bring me the money back he owed me, but he never did! I also told my lawyer I know it was wrong for me to gamble my hard-earned money away, money that I had gotten from washing cars and cutting grass, but I trusted the guy. "And here's the kicker, Mr. Note," I said, "The kid that gave me the car took off before I could get his first or last name."

My lawyer looked at me as if to say, that lie was so ridiculous, but I know you believe it was good. And I know you believe you just told the greatest lie ever. Of course, I thought he was believing it. Although my criminal record was extensive at such a young age, I was still a kid who had the audacity to believe I was running game on this lawyer. Mr. Note told me the jailer would be coming to get me to take me back over to adult court. I would be able to see him and my mom then. When I got back to my cell the boys and girls was out of their cells for a recreation activity.

I saw Kenney at one of the tables. I told him I would be leaving sometime today for court and I won't be back over here. Kenney said the staff told him JC was still in the hospital, I said tell JC to save us some of those bomb drugs he getting from those doctors and nurses. And tell JC I will come and visit you cats later. A couple hours passed, then finally I was taken to the adult side of the courthouse to have my day in court. When I got into the court room, I saw my mom sitting in the back row where there was a lot of seats.

My lawyer was up in the front of the courtroom at one table that had two chairs. Several feet in between that table was another table with two men sitting behind it. I was brought into the courtroom and put down in front where my lawyer was. I heard a deputy sheriff say, "All Rise! For The Judge!" But in my thoughts, it sounded like he was saying "All Rise! Let the circus begin!" By the time they got through reading all my charges, even including charges from back in Detroit I felt they was trying to give me life. Because the judge was reading all the things that was going on in me and Jimmy's apartment: illegal guns, drugs, sex and digging up my past records could only mean this is not going to go well for me. My lawyer did interrupt the judge by saying, "Your honor we're asking that the new charges be dismissed. We have statements that do not place my client anywhere in the vicinity of the crime in question."

The prosecutor stated, "He is not in school. He has a probation violation. His record includes stolen cars, armed robbery, gang activities, breaking out of our (the state's) correctional facilities, and has been in and out of foster homes." My lawyer interrupted, "My client has a learning disability. He will be looking for a special school to enroll in. And he is also looking for a job. He doesn't even have a social security card."

The prosecutor said in a stern tone. "And he would not even have a place to stay if the court were to release him." The prosecutor said. "Because his family home was just raided, and his grandparents are up in age. Your honor where would this young man go?" My lawyer acted like he was lost for words. My lawyer asked the judge if he could approach the bench. As the judge nodded yes, the prosecutor acted like he was invited and ran up to the judge's bench too.

The judge called a 15-minute break. And now my lawyer was talking to me about taking a deal where I would be out in three months. Right now, because of my record. I was looking at some big time. More time than I have served in the past. How much time, he did know. But he knew with a deal he would have me on the street in a couple of months. I told Mr. Note to go back to where my mom was sitting at and see what she think? My mom nodded to me to take a deal. When my lawyer, the prosecutor, and I got back in front of the judge I thought to myself, I knew I was a bad kid. But I didn't think I was that bad!

When I heard the judge hand down my sentence of 0 to 48 months (0 to 4 years) in Saint Cloud Reformatory for Men all I could hear was my mother crying in the back of the courtroom. My lawyer was shaking his head. In my disbelief, the prosecutors were happily smiling. Smiling as if they had just won the lottery. While the prosecutors were picking up their legal pads and rushing out of the courtroom, the judge told my lawyer it was ok for me to visit my mother with him present for five minutes. I was upset and angry! I started cussing at my mom and yelling! I told her, "You said I was going to get out of here!" As I think back, I regret treating my mom that way.

The lawyer cut me off before I could get another word out my mouth! "Young man," He said, "You don't how lucky you are to have a mother like the mother you have." My mom was still crying. She had not stopped since the judge announced my sentence. While crying my mom was telling me how sorry she was for not being a better mother. But the lawyer kept on lecturing me, like my mom wasn't even there. The lawyer said, "You should not disrespect your mom! I don't think my mom would have pawned her diamond rings to pay the last of the $1500 dollars she owed me for representing you! Her oldest son! You should be thankful she tried. And so did I."

I didn't believe my lawyer did all he could, but I know deep down inside of me, the lawyer was right about my mom. She did her best! And if God is hearing me right now I thank him for my mom! I gave my mother a big hug! And told her not to worry. I told her, "Hug my brothers and sister for me man! I will miss them." I shook the lawyer's hand and gave my mother one last hug and kiss goodbye. I thought to myself, this time I won't let her see me cry. I will hold back all my tears. I am almost 17 year-old young man now. I am on my way, going to prison.

WHEN GOD
PLANTS A SEED

This is why I speak to them in parables, because seeing they do not see, and hearing they do not hear, nor do they understand.

—Matthew 13:13
English Standard Version (ESV)

But blessed are your eyes, for they see, and your ears, for they hear. For truly, I say to you, many prophets and righteous people longed to see what you see, and did not see it, and to hear what you hear, and did not hear it.

—Matthew 13:16
English Standard Version (ESV)

WOW! As the van pulled up to the Prison in Saint Cloud, Minnesota I was thinking to myself, this is nothing like Lino Lakes Correctional Facility (the juvenile facility) This is prison! The Saint Cloud Men's Prison made the Lino Lakes juvenile facility look like a boy's club. I was not afraid but more star struck in regards to how huge the buildings were and how high the walls looked. It felt as though the walls was looking down on me.

The barbed wire fence that surrounded the prison, seemed to stretch out for miles with no end in sight. The long tan stone steps with the long copper rails made you feel like, once you entered the inside of the big monster doors at the top of the stairs the monster doors would swallow you up. I had to stop for a moment and take-a-look around. I had to, needed to get one last glimpse of freedom. Suddenly, a voice yells out, "NO TALKING! LOOK STRAIGHT AHEAD! AND WHILE YOUR WALKING TO THE SHOWER AREA DON'T FALL OUT OF LINE! The guards barked out commands and yelled at us incoming inmates from all sides.

I'm still in disbelief that the judge thought sending a kid to prison would be rehabilitation. Me and the other guys that was also riding in the prison van, was told to put all of our clothes and belongings into a plastic bag the guard handed to each of us. Everything needed to be in the plastic bag before we got off the van. After being taken to the shower by the guards we were given only minutes to wash our bodies. After leaving the shower each of us was sprayed with what seemed like bug spray all over our body.

After coming out of the shower and being sprayed, me and the six guys I rode on the prison van with had to fall into line to receive a number. This number assigned to me and the other guys became how we will be identified until we leave here. The guards said to us, "You inmates must remember this number! This is now your name for the whole time you are here! Even if you are here for the rest of your life!" A guard said to me directly, "Is that understood 27-3!" I replied with a nod of my head as a non-verbal yes, sir that I understand.

I thought to myself, do they yell all the time?! I also thought to myself it would be good for me to be on my best behavior until I could figure out the layout of this new institution. I was wondering if this was another one of society's plans to show me that there was no hope for me on the outside? With all these thoughts rambling through my head I was given a stamped copper tag with the number I was assigned. The tags made me feel like a dog they could find easily if I tried to run.

It became crystal clear that this was a dream that I was not going to wake up from no time soon. I had never seen that many black, white, and brown people all bunched up together in my life. There were inmates walking around in different colored uniforms. Some had on blue jean shirts, paints, jackets, and white tennis shoes. Others were wearing tan khaki pants, tan khaki shirts, and brown boots.

The uniforms added a bit of color to the institutional decor of gray and hospital surgical unit green that was on the cement walls and in the prison cells which made The prison look like the inside of a graveyard burial tomb. Whether the inmate was short, muscular, fat, tall, skinny, or lanky you could tell that every one of these inmates that had on these robes of confinement was trapped in this night of the living dead graveyard called prison.

Welcome to rehabilitation almost 17 year-old. While walking down the long hallway carrying my blanket and sheets to my new home, that had no avenue. The address was your cell number, which was different from your assigned identification number. While being shown to our cells it was all eyes on us. We could hear the inmates throughout the cell block yelling and whistling at us like wolves teaming up with the devil to see who could have the first bite at you for entering into their forbidden territory.

As I heard the big clunk of the cell door opening and the rolling of a hundred steel chains running together at the same time for the cell door to easily open, the guard said, "Step into your cell. Chow will be in 30 minutes. When you hear the speaker sound off your cell door will open. Come out, stand in line, and follow the other inmates to the dining area." What went through my mind was step into the cave of uncertainty, don't ask questions, just do as you are told.

As my cell door closed behind me. I put my sheets and blanket down and sat on the steel framed bed with its thin mattress and flat pillow. I felt a sour taste come into my mouth as I wondered what's was for supper. My thoughts were interrupted by the sound of speakers and cell doors opening. Inmates began to come out their cells just like the guard explained. I heard a different kind of quietness coming from the inmates, as the shuffle of hundreds of feet marched down the long hallway to chow.

The low whispering I was hearing from in front of me and in the back of me, made it clear to me that we was not to be talking in line. And the inmates who were talking was being very careful not to get caught. Wow! The dining hall was huge! All I could see was tan, white, and blue on the floor and the walls. I heard a few people calling my name as I was getting my food from the chow line! They was waving their hands for me to come over to the table they was sitting at.

Man, I thought to myself it was so good to see friends I knew from northside and southside. I also saw a few people I knew from Saint Paul. There were a lot of cats (young men I knew) coming over to the table. I felt overwhelmed and at ease all at the same time. I never thought I would know so many people in prison. We all had one thing in common, we knew each other from the streets or from Lino Lakes.

And for some us who had been locked up before this wasn't our first rodeo. But it was the first time in an adult facility. While looking up I noticed a basketball hoop hanging from the ceiling and basketball court designs on the dining hall floor. J.B. told me they use the dining area for indoor games when we can't go out on the courtyard and for other special events. I was so busy catching up with what was going on with some of the guys I knew that chow was over with and someone was on the loud-speaker telling us to put our trays on the cart and head back to our cells.

I had not eaten hardly anything. A.J. said for me not to worry. He would make sure the guy got me something for me from the kitchen after inmates were counted. As the guards was taking a head count of each and every inmate I was making my bed and straightening out my 6 by 8 feet cell when someone flew past my cell and threw a couple of sandwiches through the cell bars. They was not wrapped up or anything. So, I took one of my court papers that the guards let me keep and I folded one of sandwiches up in the paper. I ate the other one so fast I don't remember what was in between the slices of bread.

Later when I ate the other one I found out it was ham & cheese. As I was laying back checking out my new surroundings, I felt pretty-good knowing some of the guys that was here, knew who I was. All the guys I knew in here was all around 16 and 17 years old. I know now if something went down in here I got someone watching my back.

The loud-speaker interrupted my thoughts. The person on the speaker said the cells would be open for socializing. Once the cells were opened, I found out you could only socialize with the guys that was in your cell block. I was in Cell B Block. They had a table in the hallway so that the inmates could play cards or dominoes. Inmates could also go to each other's cells and visit. A few of the guys that was at chow earlier came to my cell area. J.B., B.H., A., and M.C. gave me some books to read. Like Donald Goines and Iceberg Slim. Authors who wrote about street life. Others gave me some snacks like crackers and Tang.

Tang was an orange powder you could mix with water to make a nice orange drink. B.H. and J.B., who was from the northside of Minneapolis had given me the run-down of the prison. The do's and don'ts, the snitches, the guards that was straight up (would be truthful with you), and the inmates to watch out for. Like the ones that would cut your throat in a minute.

Then I saw a face I had not seen since I left from Detroit! It was T.L. He was a few years older than me. So, he had to be about 20 or 21. Once T.L. and I started talking the other guys left from around my cell so me and T.L. could talk. I wanted to catch up on what was going on in the Motor City (the nickname for Detroit).

T.L. always had that gangster attitude about himself. But he was also a revolutionary for his people. T.L. started out his conversation with me by saying, "Man, It's crazy back in the Motor City! Stokely Carmichael, Rap Brown, and others involved with the Black Panther Party are still doing their Black Power to the People thing. You know fighting police brutality against black people and people of color. The racial profiling is so strong there." T.L. said that people from our old neighborhood in Motor City was hollering BLACK POWER! Trying to get people to see how black people are being mistreated. Some organizations heard the black power cry and tried to create programs to help but other organizations ain't trying to hear that.

T.L. said, "So, they're (people in charge of city government and others) throwing the love and peace for our community out the window." T.L. told me about a couple of kids we ran with back in in Detroit. He said they was shot to death. "Wow!" I said, "That's sad!" Even though the shootings T.L told me about happened several years ago. They was only 14 years old when they were shot and killed.

He went on to tell me that it's all about money and drugs now. And with all the heroin and coke (cocaine) coming in from Vietnam, the gravy train (selling drugs and making money) had started. People were either getting on the train or getting crushed on the tracks. T.L. said, "I even heard there might be a black syndicate or mafia organization developing in our city" I said. Wow! Man, these white-folk is trying to stop all us from making money."

T.L. went on to tell me that him and his uncle was making one of their drug runs and got arrested on their way back from Kansas City in Albert Lee, Minnesota. They were pulled over for speeding. During the stop, the police had found a little bit of weed they had been smoking. Along with some cameras and other stolen goods in his uncle's car trunk. While T.L. and his uncle was in jail the police found out the stolen items came from a house broken into in Minneapolis. T.L. said, "I got five years for burglary."

Our conversation was interrupted by the loud-speaker. The person on the speaker said, "All inmates to return to their cells for lock up!" T.L. and I gave each other the black hand-shake and I thanked him for the info. I went into my cell with all kinds of feelings running through my mind.

As the lights went out and I could see the guard's shadow growing bigger and larger on the cell walls. The guard's keys clinging and sounding louder as his flashlight got closer to the cell I was in. The light was shining so bright in my face it was as if I was on stage and I could not see the people in the front row. I was squinting the way performers do when they are on stage and the lights are not set the way they should be.

Then I heard the sound of the guard's military footsteps marching off into the darkness. The steps never skipped a beat. As I heard the last of the footsteps fade away I knew the inmate head count was over with until the next hour. I laid down on the cold steal frame bed with the thin cushion in between that, which they called a mattress. I thought about all the events that had took place in one day which already seemed like a week.

A few of the guys I came in the van with earlier today looked kind of meek and weak. I knew from the whispering and growling we heard earlier as we were taken to our cells was meant for one of them. I knew that one of the inmates that whistled and made sounds at the new inmates was feeling like he had won a prize. And was preparing to tell a new inmate, "You're my woman now! And I better not see you looking any other man in here!"

And then I heard from another cell, "You remember what happened under the dining table at chow?" I heard a faint squeaky voice answer back, "Yes, just don't hurt me." Wow! I thought to myself in this chamber of hell only the strong survive. When did the hunter become the wanted? Even though my night in this place was a little uncomfortable and I had seen men behave as women os they would not be killed in jail and other joints I've been in, I never heard it sound so cold, so bold, so vicious.

To get that cold-bloodedness out of my mind I started thinking about home. Missing my grandmother's cooking. During my thoughts of home, I was awakened by a lot of cells unlocking. And the cell blocks lights coming on. There was new faces of guards walking up and down the cell block floors and inmates dressed in white moving real fast. Moving like they was on their way to put out a fire without a water hose!

I asked the guy in the cell next to me what was going on. He said it was the guards changing shifts and inmates going to the kitchen to set up for breakfast. He told me we had about an hour before our cells would be opened, I brushed my teeth and used the potato sack (old potato sacks were made of burlap) looking wash cloth to wash my face in the sink of unforgiveness. The sink that sat next to the toilet seat of no hope that would just keep on flushing away my freedom.

I took the tin cup that sat on the sink and put some of the orange powder in it. I pushed the button that was connected to the sink and let the stream of cold water fill the cup. I stirred the orange flavored water with my finger. It felt good going down my throat. Speaking of Tang. I think this was same kind of drink the astronauts used while going up in space. Maybe they will have some kind of food I can get from canteen that comes from outer space too. Like flying hamburgers or something.

My thoughts was interrupted by cell doors opening up for breakfast. A kite (a note on a piece of paper) was given to me by one of the guards. I was going to meet with the psychiatrist and correctional facility staff for orientation after I am done eating. It felt good to have some coffee, hard toast, eggs, and oatmeal in my belly. It was good talking to T.L., J.B., M.B. and some of the other guys in the dining hall. But this time I ate and was not missing a beat.

Some of guys was telling me about the lightweight jobs and the heavy jobs that I might get assigned to. I really wasn't paying attention though. The fact was I didn't like any kind of manual labor, so I didn't intend to do hard work. And if assigned correctional staff would soon find out I am not good at jobs that required hard labor. As I left the dining area one of the guards escorted me to a different part of the prison. I was lead to a room where three people were sitting.

I didn't know if it was the warden top guard or what. I did know one of them had to be the psychiatrist just by the way he was talking. The top guard was running down (explaining) all the rules, while the other man was just writing stuff on a piece of paper. At first I was thought I was going to be assigned to the license plate plant in the prison. This is where Minnesota state license plates were made. But since I was 17 with no high school diploma, I was allowed to go to classes for my GED.

My work assignment was to work in the laundry part of the prison. The person taking notes in this meeting asked me, did I have any questions. I thought to myself why would, you ask me that like I'm not locked up or something and had a choice in what was being said in this 'meeting.' And before I could get the word, no out of my mouth good, someone in the meeting told the guard to take me to the laundry plant and put me to work.

When I got to the laundry I met the person in charge. He put me to work taking blue jeans out of one of the gigantic washer while having one of the inmates show me how everything was done in the laundry area. There was a few friends I knew that worked in the laundry. So, I learned the ropes quick. Pretty soon I was walking around the prison with pressed khakis and blue jeans with creases in them.

As time went on the days seemed like months and the months seemed like years. Kenney got sent up here with a fin! (explain this word) meaning he got five years. Kenney told me before he left from up under the clock (courthouse jail) back in Minneapolis he found out why we never saw J.C. again while we in jail. 'Cause he was dead from an overdose. At least that's was what one of the staff told him.

Man! I was sorry to hear that. J.C. was a good kid. It's funny how being incarcerated can make you grow up real fast. It can make the young grow into men. And men grow wiser before their time. A lot of things was going on was on all around the world. It was 1971 and my friend Walter who used to be in my gang was sending me letters. Along with another friend of mine, A.D. They was both in the Marines serving in the Vietnam War.

They was writing and telling me here they was fighting for America, but they still was not allowed to eat or sleep in the same barracks as white Marines. Walter said he did not understand the whole war thing. And a lot of soldiers are getting strung out on heroin and other drugs. Walter said they are dying over here (Vietnam) for nothing! White and black alike are dying side by side. By each other! And I still can't go into a white establishment 'cause of the color of my skin! It just ain't right!

I wrote Walter back and told him that the Temptations and another singer named Edwin Starr had songs about war released in the early 1970's. I told Walter I think this was the way the singers was rebelling against the war. Walter wrote back and agreed with me. Speaking for myself I had my own war going on up here in prison. My temper was getting the best of me. I was getting into fights. I was shanked (cut with a homemade knife). They make shanks out of almost anything in here. And a shank can cut almost everything as good as a knife.

After I was shanked I was looking at my guts hanging out of my stomach and one guard said to another guard, "Hurry up and get him to the infirmary (prison clinic and hospital) so they can get him a band-aid. T.L. was seeing the change in me. This man-made tomb wasn't rehabilitating me! This prison was teaching me how to be a better criminal. In the infirmary I got a few stitches and was given some pills for the pain before I was sent back into population (returned to cell block with the rest of the inmates).

Not long after I got shanked a few of us were transferred to Stillwater (another adult prison facility) after a paperwork mix up. So, some of the kids who were not 21, but only 18, went to Stillwater (or The Water as it was called by inmates). My stay in The Water was short but I got a chance to see some of my grandfather's friends. They would say, "Young blood (young man), you don't want to be here to long or for any numbers of years 'cause, this can be the land of no return."

All I can say about Stillwater is nothing but walls, walls, walls, cells, cells, cells, and bars of bars and more bars. Definitely, a house of hell! Back in Saint Cloud Prison I was again at a fork in the road. My thoughts were changing. I was beginning to think about the mistreatment of black people in our country. I was beginning to see why education was important. Something was happen to me.

The prison provided inmates with recreation which gave some a brief moment away from being locked up. We were able to play football, baseball, and basketball in the prison courtyard. But inmates also knew don't get too comfortable in any particular place in prison. Being too relaxed could mean, being dead. The slightest disagreement could get you shanked or put in solitary confinement. In prison you could get it from all sides; prison administrators (warden, psychiatrist, social worker), prison guards, and/or inmates.

To tap into our humanity, we black inmates started our own black culture groups. The black culture group was big on knowledge. And I believe prison administrators agreed to let black inmates have the group to keep them calm and give them something productive to work on. The black culture group was even able to have banquets on special occasions.

The only reason why I joined the black culture group was because A.C. wanted me to join his Muslim group. But my argument to A.C. regarding joining the black culture group was that I just couldn't see myself being locked up in this prison and only living on crackers and honey. I liked pork chops, mashed potatos and gravy too much. I also told A.C. if he didn't want his tray at chow time just let me know. And he could give me all his bacon too.

A.C. started laughing and said, "He don't want me to poison myself with the devil's food." I told A.C., "Look at it this way, by the time you give your bacon to me it will be already be cooked crispy. That means the snake and/or devil will be dead enough to eat." We both started laughing. I did agreed to read the book A.C. gave me by Malcolm X called, "The End of White World Supremacy."

As my prison time went on I adapted to this new way of living, to change my life. With all the criminal activity going on around me; death, suicide, unjust treatment of inmates by prison guards, it was hard not to be drawn into the anger. Pulled into disagreements that could turn into major fights. And even being angered by guards who wanted me to fall for their petty attempts to make me angry so they would have a reason to beat me.

I remember myself and another inmate, a friend of mine; T.M. were dragged out of our cells and beaten up by guards who were in their riot gear. I was beaten for nothing. However, the beating was not the end of this mistreatment. I was chained, shackled, stripped of my clothes and with only my underwear left on, I was tossed in the prison hole (solitary confinement); like some animal.

As I was thrown into the hole the guards told me I was charged with inciting a riot. Then all I heard was the steel door being slammed shut behind me. The darkness fell upon my eyes. As I tried to adjust them to see my new surroundings all I saw was cold, hard brick block looking back at me. The old rusty toilet and sink was the only thing that stood out in the blackness.

The brick slab was very cold to my body as I sat on it trying to gather my thoughts. I don't know if I was physically hurt or not. What I know is I was numb. I was feeling a kind of pain that I never felt before! I thought to myself I don't know what part of this is supposed to be rehabilitation. The only thing I could feel in my heart, my mind and my soul, was HATE! ANGER! RESENTMENT!

But it's funny, 'cause it was not a black or white hate, but a system hate! It was questioning a system that could lock up a kid with a troubled and dysfunctional home life. And instead of offering help to me and my family they kept sending me to bigger more crowded prisons. Until I was finally a kid in an adult prison facility.

I believe I was getting picked on by the guards 'cause I was now using my mind instead of my fists. The older cats in the black culture group had me learning and reading more about who I was. Who was I was always a question I wrestled with. I knew I was black. What I didn't know, is what that meant. Black in America was always seen as negative, stupid, and a body that should be used for labor.

I had read a lot of books while in prison. But the two that stuck out the most was the 1964 book "Before The Mayflower" by Lerone Bennett Jr. This book was about the struggles and triumphs of black Americans. The second book was a 1970 book by P.M. Wilson called, "Simplified Swahili". I had started learning the Swahili language and even took on a Swahili name, Jawara Kambon.

As I became more culturally knowledgeable, I felt like I was a human being. Like I was somebody. It was the viewing my black history in a way that I could understand it. It awakened my consciousness. I started being very outspoken on how a lot of systemic tools was being used as a hammer of injustice and all the nails that were used to break down our minds, bodies, and souls, bit by bit. It was crooked and it was wrong! And what I found out was if you spoke about it you would be punished.

I thought to myself here I am, 18 years old about to be 19 and I am trapped in a three-way system. A system that sees me a sub-human. The three-way system to me is: society, the law, and inmates. All of which depend on white people to decide if you as a black person are worthy to live. Worthy to fully participate in society. And worthy to be considered human.

You might think prison is the cruelest of all these systems. However, I would disagree, American society is the cruelest of these systems because it's society that has created the other two systems which have no compassion for people who look like me. The cruelty in prison did not start in prison it started in society that created the prison. It's a system that leaves no room for error for black people and quite honestly poor people or anyone society believes is different. It's a system that has created a never-ending circle of death.

As my anger and hate begins to subside, I took another look around the dark dungeon also known as solitary confinement that I was in. Only this time I let my heart take on a different attitude. I can now see through the darkness of this dungeon. My young mind was hearing the words, I Am Not A Product Of Failure! I asked myself, Who Am I? Again, I thought about the books I read, "Before The Mayflower" and "Simplified Swahili". I thought about my grandmother and the words she often spoke to me. "If God is for me who can be against me!"

What a bright light of understanding that came to me. I began crying because I knew the light in solitary confinement just became brighter in a chamber of no hope. The seed had been planted in my soul, I AM JAWARA KAMBON! I AM A MIGHTY AFRICAN KING! No matter how long I was to be locked up in this hell hole, I will stay strong. Even as I am given food through a slot that was no larger than a mail slot on a metal door. Even as what I am fed is a small portion of food twice a day on a paper tray and spoon that had to be returned through the mail slot or I would not get my next meal. Even as I sit in this hole and could not tell if it was day or night, I knew I would not let this moment get the best of me.

I used my regular population schedule to guide my body and my mind about what time it might be. To pass the time I would do push-ups, sit-ups, and sing old songs to myself I would even make up my own songs. I would also run-in place and shadow box in the dim light that was left in the cell after the guard opened, up the small mail slot to check on you. I'm sure they did that to see if someone in solitaire had committed suicide. But if administrators knew putting people in solitary confinement could move them to suicide why would they subject them to that. Because they view us (inmates) as sub-human.

After what seemed like years I was finally released from the hole, 40 days later. Next I was lead to segregation. Segregation was in D Block. What the inmates called The Dog-House. Once In D Block I still had the blindfold in my hand that I received coming out of solitary confinement to protect my eyes. You are given a blindfold coming out of solitary confinement because coming out of darkness after 40 days into light immediately can damage the eyes.

My eyes were slowly becoming adjusted to the light. Segregation was another lock up within the prison where inmates leaving solitary confinement had to stay until they went to court. What was referred to by the inmates as kangaroo court. Because no matter what you did or what proof you had to share regarding why you were sent to solitary you would not be heard. You would only be told what you did and how the matter would be handled.

This kind of court was a joke. And most of the time you (the inmate) was found guilty. While in segregation it felt good to take a shower. Yes, I was in solitary for 40 days with the only light coming from a mail slot used to bring me food. And was not able to shower or clean myself up. It felt good to be able to talk to others that had also spent time in solitary. I was also able to have a couple of books in the cell.

After my stint (time) in kangaroo court I was released back into the regular population for good behavior. T.M. (the guy who was also accused of starting a riot) was also back in population. The first song I heard from an inmate's cell was "Maggie May" by Rod Stewart was a cool white dude who had a lot of hit songs in the 1970's. As I passed by the cell playing this song I stopped to talk to the inmate. His name was Bill. Each cell had an outlet that allowed inmates to listen to music with ear plugs that were connected to the cell wall.

Bill and I became good friends. He encouraged me to join Toastmasters. A public speaking club. I won a trophy in a competition. All my prison friends was proud of me. I spoke about Frederick Douglass an American Slave. I was even more excited when my African name, Jawara Kambon was put on the trophy.

As time went on I saw my friends leave the prison and even saw a couple of them come back. I didn't understand why I was still sitting here. Even female friends and family I was corresponding with was wondering when was I coming home. I had ran out patience listening to these new case managers who had just got to the prison and was trying to analyze me. They acted like they had been knowing me for years.

Here it is 1972 and I am still in prison. Some of my friends who had murder charges would be soon coming up for their parole soon. So why am I still here? As I was going back and forth on this in my mind, I decided right then and there I would do the rest of my 4 years, then I would be out and be done with this wretched prison. Even as I am writing this I am thinking about my friends who made it out of prison. C. J. who is now a prominent bishop in the community and T. M. who is also doing great work in the community. I am also thinking about a few others who were trapped in a world of the forgotten children. Kenney, J.L., J.C., T. L., A.J., and the ones who died behind the walls and bars of uncertainty (prison).

I think about Walter and A.D. and how the Vietnam War had messed up their minds so bad with the military racism, fighting a war for others fighting to be free while black soldiers were not free and black people were fighting the civil rights battle in America and the drugs they became hooked on. But also came back to a country that called itself the land of the free while not just mistreating black people but lynching them, sending dogs to bite them while they peacefully protested, spit on them while they peacefully protested, sprayed them with fire hoses while they peacefully protested, killed them via drowning beating and cutting of their private parts. Fighting for freedom in Vietnam. Give me a break.

No wonder black soldiers came back to the land of the free with post dramatic stress. Quite honestly, they had it before they left. T.A. made it through the war and chose to stay in Germany. He still lives there to this day. I guess black really is beautiful in Germany. Because black beauty in America still remains a question mark for many. And sadly, part of the many are black.

As I sit here crying silently in my pain! I know I need to continue my story. So, time went on with my everyday life of prison living. Eventually, I went back up in front of the parole board. I was staying out of trouble. I did good on my General Equivalent Diploma (GED). And I felt I had been quote, "Rehabilitated and could now be a productive member of society". The parole board consisted of case managers, a psychiatrist, the warden, the commissioner with department of corrections, and anyone else that had the power to approve or deny my case.

I went to the Parole Review Board about every 6 months. And now I am 19 years old. I really didn't care at this point if the Parole Review Board granted my parole or not. I could only be held in prison for two more years if the board decided not to grant my parole. So, the only thing on my mind was BLACK POWER! LET MY PEOPLE GO!

Some weeks had passed, and I still hadn't heard from the parole board. It was February 19 72 when a guard came out to the courtyard and said, Go back to your cell, pack up your letters and pictures because you are going home." As slow as time passed while I was here, suddenly; everything was moving kind of fast.

I met with a case manager that told me I would be living with this guy and his family that was supposed to be another stepdad. He and he my mom would be picking me up. I was both surprised and curious. But didn't ask any questions. I was ready to go home, wherever home was, just as long as it was away from here. Questions could wait. I went to the same room where I was checked into prison almost two years ago.

I was given the plastic bag that had my clothes in them when I came to prison. I had been in prison for several years as a teenager, so it was no surprise to me when my shoes didn't fit. The other clothes I had when I arrived did not fit either. Can you imagine being in prison as a kid and when you are released to your family the clothes you had when you arrived do not fit when you are leaving? The clothes I had made me look like an over grown clown, but thanks to the state I be walking out the prison with the new khakis and boots that I was currently wearing.

I was given three pairs of socks, 3 pairs of underwear and $300 dollars in my pocket. Only a few hundred yards more and I would be free. My stomach was churning. I could feel the butterflies as I heard the sounds of thousands of chains rolling, unlocking and slamming while the gates behind me were closing with me on the outside of those gates. Just a few more steps I told myself. Then I heard a guard say, "GOOD LUCK!" And another guard said, You'll be back!"

Then came the sound of clanging, banging, and rolling of chains again. As the last steel bars closed behind me the big monster door that looked like it would swallow me up when I entered the prison opened up its ugly mouth to release me and spit me back out into society, rehabilitated? I went down the last step and touched my foot on the ground of doubt.

I did not feel free at all. It was something about what that guard had said about me coming back that tugged at me. I questioned myself, Had I not done my time? Am I not free? Is my time just beginning? Does freedom come with a price?

I smiled to myself as I took one last look at the prison. No! I won't be back! The seed of knowledge had been planted.

EVEN THUGS, HUSTLERS, & PLAYERS TAKE A LUNCH BREAK

GETTING OUT OF prison and coming back out into the community takes a little time. Getting use to the changes that occurred out in the streets while I was away took a minute. There was black movements (organizations, groups, and individuals fighting for the black community's civil rights). These fights for civil rights were going on all over the Twin Cities (the nickname for Minneapolis and Saint Paul) and across the nation. Some people talking were about black power. Others were in Muslim Organizations selling newspapers and bean pies to fund their cause, get in touch with people to share their beliefs, and move their black power agenda forward.

The church was saying amen! And the people that was working hard paycheck to paycheck were owning less and being heard even more less. In other words, the poor was getting poorer, the rich was getting richer, and people of color were just fighting to be treated as human. In the middle of all the black power, white control battles were *My* individual and very real-world struggles. I understood the nation and my community had their struggles, but at this time my young mind could only grapple with my own struggles.

A friend of my mom's had gotten me a job at a gas station. Located on Park & Lake St. on the south side of Minneapolis. I was also given the first three month's rent on an efficiency apartment on 32nd and Park Avenue South. I thought to myself not bad for a kid who went into prison at 17 years old, got out at 19 years old. Now this same man gave me a 1963 white Cadillac convertible. The man who I will just call W.H. said he would keep the Cadillac and insurance in his name until I got my driver's license.

W.H. told me, "If you get stopped just tell them you're my son." At the time I did not know how close to the truth this statement was. But, back to the current moment. It felt good to have my own place. And even though I lived only a few blocks away from the new job that was set up for me, I would still be late for work. My mindset did not understand being on time. I was not introduced to being on time until I went to prison. And now that I'm out I have very little interest in being on someone else's time clock.

About a year later, October 1973, I had got a letter in the mail from the State of Minnesota. I was off parole. The letter also stated that I had my citizenship back. I thought to myself, got my citizenship back?! That's funny, I didn't even know I had lost my citizenship when I went to prison. I also thought, oh well; I don't have an identification card or driver's license, social security card, or birth certificate either. I'm a newly restated citizen, who didn't know he lost his status as a citizen, with no way to identify myself. How's this going to work?

I attempted a few times to get my birth certificate but no such luck. My mom, the city of Minneapolis, and no one else I asked seemed to know what happened to my birth certificate. The birth certificate was needed to get a driver's license or at least a State of Minnesota I.D. card. As I'm thinking about my identification situation my girlfriend was yelling and honking her horn. I heard her outside my apartment window yelling for me to come downstairs.

We was going to some kind of Black African meeting over in north Minneapolis at The Way (a community organization). My girl-friend T.L. and I had knew each other as teens. She was heavy off into the African Movement. She is still, to this day helping people of color in Minnesota and across the country with programs she has created. I knew in my heart T.L. and I would eventually break up because education and black power was her passion. At the time my only passion was taking care of me.

Even though I had my own spot (apartment) I would still see my brothers and sister from time to time. They was all back at home too. They all went into foster care when our mom and stepdad's home was raided. They were also involved in activities that were criminal to some and survival to others. My sister was a gangster. One of my brother's was making a better than average living as a pimp in California. And my other brother committed armed robberies but also played football while in school.

One day while working at the gas station I just happen to look across the street at the car wash and saw Destiny. The Catholic school girl I was trying to get with before I got locked up. I knew that tall light brown skinned slim frame anywhere. The dress that she had on was below her knees. It made you know loud and clear that what was between her legs was unforbidden territory.

She was getting into her car as I yelled out her name and waved for her to come across the street to the gas station. I told Lonnie to cover for me, while I watched Destiny getting out of the car. Her beautiful long black hair shined like a black satin scarf blowing in the afternoon wind. Her smile and turquoise looking eyes made her look like a Puerto Rican princess.

We hugged and embraced each other. Wow, I thought to myself she looks good. The thug in me just wanted to grab her, kiss her, and make the deepest of deep love to her. But I respected her boundaries and just gave her another passionate hug. Destiny said she was glad to see me and she wanted to write but her mother told her she didn't want her to have anything to do with a hoodlum. Even though she knew you were innocent of what you were being accused of.

My mom said you was still a gangster and a thug! Cause she heard about you through other people. Destiny said, "Lee I still was praying for you all the time and I never forgot you." Just as Destiny said that Lonnie was waving and yelling at me that the boss was coming so I needed to get back to work. Before I left, I asked Destiny if we could hook up later at the donut shop where I took her to lunch when I last saw her. Destiny said, "No Sir Lee, you owe me some real food." Then I said, "How about Currents Restaurant that was down a ways from Regina High School where you use to go to school?"

Destiny agreed, so we set up a time to meet, 7:00 p.m. I got off work at 4:00 p.m. so that would give me time to clean myself up. Being on time may be a priority this evening. When I got back inside the gas station Lonnie was saying to me, "Man, that girl is not your type! She don't even look like she wears hot pants (very short shorts). We need to go down to the Chicken Shack after work where the real dames (girls, women) are at and get something to eat."

I laughed at Lonnie and said I got something else to do this evening. While he was going out to pump gas into a customer's car, I thought to myself, dang I have to go to some kind meeting with T.L. at her university campus tonight. I have to call T.L. and let her know I'm not feeling well. Once I called T.L. I could tell she was sad that I could not make it to the meeting. But she shared she wanted me to feel better. Before we hung up the phone she said, "Power to the people my JAWARA. I love you. "Power to the people! I love you too." I said back to her.

It was nice seeing Destiny that evening. We laughed and talked a lot. For the first time in a long time I felt really, happy. I haven't felt like this since my relationship with Jackie. T.L. was good to me and was a good woman but there was something about Destiny that brought out the good out in me. She didn't care about my past hustler and thug life. She told me all that mattered is that we found each other again, and we can start fresh.

She was not seeing no one. I told her I was not seeing anyone either. Here I was with my 6 feet, 175-pound frame telling a real big lie. Acting like a guy who tells his friends about the two-hundred-pound fish that got away. I told myself, I wasn't really seeing another women 'cause T.L. was not sitting here in front of me at the moment. After I justified to myself cheating on T.L., Destiny and I officially sealed our 'exclusively' dating one another with a hug and a gigantic kiss as we left the restaurant.

The next morning Lonnie and my boss from the gas station was surprised to see me on time. They started clapping their hands as if they was in shock. I knew Destiny was good for me. T.L. and the black power moments I had with her was going ok. But I was living a double life. Juggling two girlfriends at one time. Black power movement with one and ordinary citizen with the other. But I knew street life was still tugging at me because I needed/wanted more money.

By now C.J. and Kenney was out of the joint, along with a few others I knew. Some of the guys had went back to strong-armed robbery, some stayed in the gangs they were in before they went to prison, and some of them was off into the mack (pimpin) game. Still, others were drug dealing. Some of the girls I knew from junior high and high school was off into prostitution. People I knew were doing what they could and what they knew to make a dollar.

One of my brothers who had came back from California was staying with my family. He was deep into the mack game. He would stop by the gas station and say, "Whenever you are ready to make some real money let me know." My other brother who got out of Red Wing (a juvenile detention facility) was even crazier than me. He was a straight up a bank robber. He didn't believe robbing stores would be enough money for him.

My sister was off into the hustler game as well. I started falling off the black power thing 'cause a lot of people of color was making it seem like either you had the money to handle your business or you didn't. Which in my mind meant the rich was getting richer and the poor was getting poorer. And at this time I was one of the poorer. That was going to have to change.

So, the winter of 1975 I took my brother's advice. I needed to make some real money and I started doing my little hustling, dealing drugs and selling hot items (stolen goods) here and there at the gas station. I kept the gas station job for a little while, while I was hustling but knew the hustle was going to take more of time if I was going to make any real money. And the more I was seeing the fancy cars that the players was driving, the clothes, and diamonds they was wearing; plus the ladies of the night wrapped around their arms which reminded me of a delicious box of candy that could only be opened by the best taster, I knew pumping gas would not satisfy my craving for cars, money, and women.

My thought process just made me want to become more of a pimp. Not just a pimp, but 'The Pimp,' like Iceberg Slim and Donald Goines who I read about in prison. I was still off into my thoughts while watching the players get out their cars across the street from the gas station at the car wash. Lonnie still had not come back from lunch. It was getting late and I wanted Lonnie to get back before the boss came around.

We always covered for each other at work. Just as I noticed it was getting late, I saw Lonnie. He pulled up and as he was getting out of his car, I saw him straightening out his work shirt and trying to wipe off the lip stick that was on his collar. He claimed it was a new kind of barbecue sauce. I smiled as he told this lie because the barbecue sauce didn't match the chicken crumbs that was still on his work shirt.

I said, "Man your wife is going to get you if you keep on tricking with those ladies of the night up at the Chicken Shack." Lonnie said, "What you talking about Jawara or cawara or whatever you call yourself." Lonnie took a joint out his pocket looked around, lit it up, took a puff and handed it to me. With smoke still coming out of his mouth, he said, "Jawara! Jawara! don't you know, don't you know; even thugs, hustlers, and players takes a lunch break."

I had to smile when Lonnie said that. I had never thought about that before. But for some reason what he had just said to me was going to stick with me and change my life. I thought it might change my life forever. Maybe it was important to me because it made me look at the hustling and pimping game in a way I had never thought of before. And that is I would be able to control my own thing, on my own time, in my own way.

I knew I was getting ready to rewrite the players' book. And put some capital, G-A-M-E into the street game. And one thing I learned about the streets at a very young age was If You Don't Respect The Game, The Game Is Not Going To Respect You! My aunt in Detroit told me that at eleven years old. I never forgot it and I lived by that code.

THE OPEN GATE: WHEN PLAYERS FALL

"Enter by the narrow gate. For the gate is wide and the way is easy[a] that leads to destruction, and those who enter by it are many. For the gate is narrow and the way is hard that leads to life, and those who find it are few.

—Matthew 7:13–14
English Standard Version (ESV)

As I was combing my hair in the mirror, getting ready to go out to the club, I was thinking about all the women and children in my world. I had married Destiny some time back. We had a one-year-old son. I also had a mistress. We had a one-year-old baby girl and another baby on the way. Yes, the mistress was pregnant, again

Oh me oh my! What's a player to do? I loved both women. I had a couple of women working the streets for me, and with my wife Destiny and my mistress B.A., hating each other's guts; I thought life was going pretty good. With them hating one another there might be a lot of fighting but not a lot of girl talk which could lead to all my secrets being shared. And we can't have that!

I would run into T.L. every once in a while, (the girl I was dating who was involved in all the black power movement stuff and attending college). She was still going to school and was still off into helping people of color in the movement. Even with our break-up, when she found out I was cheating on her, we still remained good friends. Hair done, immaculately dressed; off to the club!

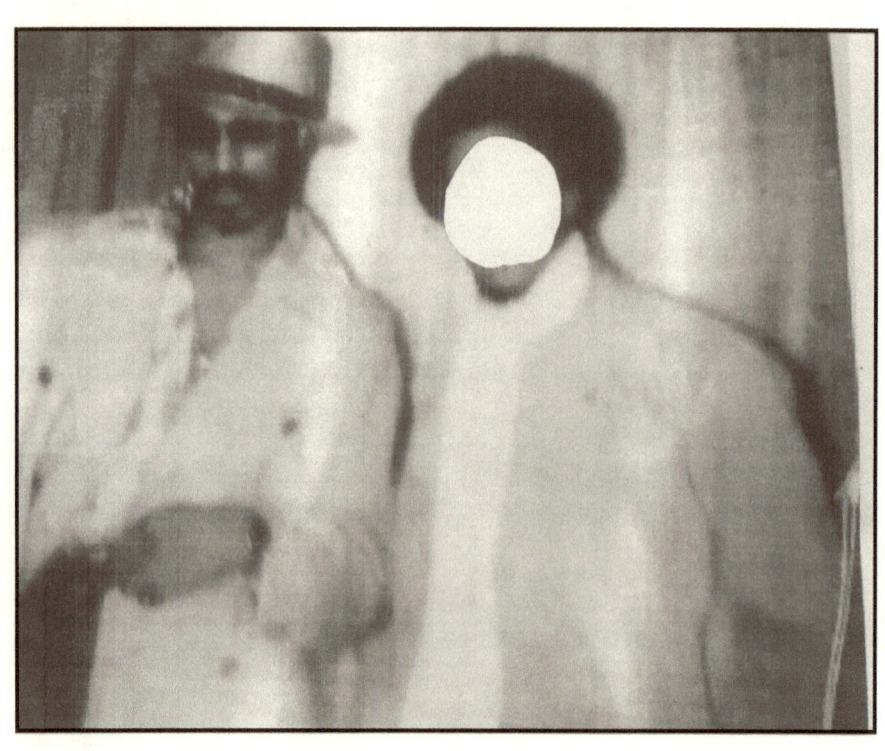

Ed Roy at the club

While at the club hanging out with the other players and watching some of the hustlers shooting pool, or just walking around watching the boosters trying to sell you some hot items like stolen watches, fake diamonds and/or jewelry I was always scanning the room to make sure something wasn't about to pop off. Because the club could be a place of leisure or a place of trouble. So it was always good for me to be aware of my surroundings.

I always saw the club as one of many gates to temptation that can lead to hell. Gates of hell for your mind, that is. Don't get me wrong, the clubs can be for people to go out dance, drink and have fun. Those are the people who can step in and step out of the gates of temptation with ease. But remember, the idle mind is a playground for devil. And the clubs provide the kind of temptation that makes one believe the gateway to hell is fun. What the devil does not provide for you is that fun can quickly become a nightmare. And when the devil plays with your head, he plays for keeps, and wants your soul.

However, when I was fully into the game, I was hardly worried about what the devil wanted with my soul. Finding another lady to add to my current collection was where my head was. So, while in the club waiting for my ladies to come in with my money, I had some time on my hands. This down time in the club gave me more time to get more acquainted with the criminology of the player's game. How a player thought, how a player talked, how a player moved through the club to bring all attention and eyes in the club on him.

Attention in the player's game is important. You want men to think you're cool and you want women to think your smooth. Your presence in any room should let men know you ain't to be f*&^% with. And let women know, I am the man you want to be with. It's this way of thinking that brings the devil into direct contact with what he wants, your soul. And he had mine. I could hear the devil saying, "Stick with me and I will give you the player's cookbook with all its devilish tricks and ingredients."

My African name which I received from the older cats (men) in prison Jawara Kambon stood for peace, love, and understanding. But now that I have delved fully back into the streets those words did not come out my mouth no more. And when they did the only meaning behind them was for my gain, not for love of the other person. Black power turned to green power. And sadly the green power suffocated the black power. I just could not do both. I needed money, wanted money, and went back into the only way I knew to make the money. I wanted to get me the things I thought I needed. And the street game was the only way I knew how to make that happen.

And as the old saying goes, it's better for me to have money and not need it, then to need money and not to have it. And I wanted all the women, money, and cars I could get by any means necessary. As my stable (ladies of the night) grew to five, my family grew as well. I now had three kids. My son born by my wife, two girls by B.A. who I was living with, another baby on the way by another mistress; and hanging out with my ladies who worked for me at night was enough to keep any man busy.

I had women everywhere. Women whom I dated. A woman I was married to. Women working for me. Women who were my girlfriends. And women who were my wife-in-laws (women who are somewhere between a wife and a girlfriend). But even with all the drugs, stylish clothes, cars, money, and women; there was never enough! I was becoming more dangerous in the street game.

I was hanging people (tricks, johns) off balconies for not paying my ladies' their money after they had sex with them. Because their money was my money. And let me be clear no one played with my money. I was going crazy! I just knew the devil was laughing at me. I just knew he was saying. "Don't worry about it. Its all part of the player's game. This isn't your suicide mission! It's your—don't F*&% with me mission." That's how the devil keeps you hanging on making you believe this is about your survival. And nothing should come before that.

The six to seven-hundred-dollar cocaine habit I had didn't make my conversations with the devil enlightening, they made me bolder. They made me feel as though I ruled the world. However, feeling as though I ruled the world came at a price because I could not feel that way without drinking countless pints of alcohol which fed my angry attitude, insatiable lust, and uncontrollable anger.

I was an active participant in beating the women I knew. Beating them down physically and mentally with my lies while pounding my fist into their faces and telling them I love them. While hearing the devil say, "Stop your crying player! I am giving you everything you asked for. You walked through the gate. I did not drag you. I simply introduced you to the game and you did not just enjoy it, you reveled in it." The devil also shared, "I already told you I was not here to play with you player! I'm here for your soul and nothing less." Then the devil left my head, and as he was leaving, he smiled a devilish grin because he knew he had me in the palm of his hands.

As the devil was wrapping up his utterings in my head, I could hear myself say, "I'll see all you hustlers and players tomorrow." I was almost 22 years old. And even though I was having conversations with the devil I thought my life was going good. I thought I was living life as a player should. I was doing a great deal of traveling which included being on the run from law enforcement. I got greedy, which meant hustling was not enough to take care of my needs. The more many I made the more money I needed to keep up my cocaine habit and the lifestyle I was living.

In trying to keep up with my monetary wants I went on a caper (robbery) with a couple of guys I knew from different joints (jails) I had been in. The capers these cats were involved in usually dealt with stolen credit cards and forged checks. I remember me and J.N. in a car speeding down Broadway and Emerson in North Minneapolis while being chased by the police. We jumped out of the car and started running. I had on an off-white cream leisure suit that had a lot of stretch to the material. I also had on a Godfather Dobbs Hat. The outfit I was wearing seemed like it gave me extra running speed. Cause when I took the hat off my head and had it in my hand (the way a relay runner would hold a baton) it was like I was running with the wind.

Although I still ended up getting caught it took a minute for them to catch me. But I wasn't locked up for long. I quickly had one of my girls call my lawyer up and bail me out. After being charged with theft by check and forgery I left all the risky crime alone and stayed in the business of being a gentleman of leisure (a pimp), with my stand-up (loyal) ladies of the evening. Although I gave up traveling related to check forgery, I did continue to travel, going across state lines with my ladies. We went to New York, Atlantic City, New Jersey, Oklahoma, Milwaukee, Kansas City, Tennessee, and East Saint Louis.

I had several ladies in my entourage now. My ladies were diversified. They danced in the clubs on the pole, they were boosters (stole luxury clothing and other high-end items) for my ladies who were working the tricks and johns. We were a business and it worked for us. I also had ladies who walked the streets and worked the motel rooms. It was more dangerous for these ladies because they would be in a lot of places, they knew nothing about. I didn't either. So they would have to be careful and depend a lot on their street skills and wits to get them through a situation. Whatever the situation might be. But my ladies knew the night can carry many surprises and they were always prepared to expect the unexpected.

But in situations my ladies and I always knew to keep our cool. My mornings usually started out with a stiff drink of alcohol; shots of Tanqueray Gin and orange juice. Often followed by a few snorts of cocaine up my nose. This morning ritual often made the rubbish of last night slip away from my head and left me with a cool ice sickle feeling that refreshed my brain. Giving me a feeling like I had early morning sex.

I took a shower and told my lady star, (a lady who was in charge of my other ladies) to pay our motel bill while I got dressed. We needed to stop at one of the truck-stops in Austin Minnesota to pick up two of my other ladies that were making out with the truck drivers all night. Once the work was done we had $8000.00. Which was not a bad haul for a few nights on the road. Now it's back to Minneapolis. The 1976 winter air was fresh. The sky was clear and sunny and as my Cadillac floated down the highway like a car that was on a white pearl diamond sled, we did not feel one bump on the road while driving.

I felt pretty good as I took another drag off the cigarette I was smoking. While smoking and driving I was thinking about the street game. I knew from the pimp book I read called *The Mack.*, which became a 1973 movie. Referring back to that movie and thinking back on how I am building this business convinced me that I am good at what I do. The player game was real and anyone who lived and played the life-style can tell you its not as easy as people think. But I made it look easy.

From Minnesota to New York the police was coming down hard on prostitutes and players. One reason I believed this was happening was that Minnesota was still a young state to the game. So, there was a lot of money to be made all around. There was especially a lot of money to be made for those dealing heroin (which was popular due to the Vietnam War, veterans wanted to forget the atrocities they saw while fighting the war) and cocaine on the rise.

Minnesota was pimps and prostitutes, meal ticket to riches via sex trafficking, which was at an all-time high. Although as bad as I thought I was I found out different regions ran different game. I was getting too full of myself, which 20 year- olds tend to do. Well, I most definitely learned my lesson outside the state of Minnesota when I lost two of my ladies to another women who was a pimp. She put a dent in my reputation with the ladies I had and ladies who wanted to work with me. That woman who took my women not only ticked me off, she embarrassed me as well. I knew I had to step up my game. And I knew the way to step up my game was to take down this outlaw (prostitute who was working without a pimp).

I would have to show the outlaw there could only be one king. And this king will not be sharing the pimp throne with anyone. I gave the outlaw a sexual taste of what a king can do.

With that taste I gained three ladies. They began working for me. Which worked for me, because the lady that stole some women from me took two. So now I'm up one. That's the education of the streets. And now I have a street-smart lady staying on top of my other ladies. It made good sense, and even better it made good business sense.

Life was good in the land of players. That old slew foot Satan had kept his promise. I was making my money! Yes, there were ups and downs; but as long as I was making my money the downs could be dealt with. I often wondered if any other players, ladies of the evening, or hustlers could hear Satan's laughter the way I could. We had just got back in town, when another player had pulled my coat (spoke to me) and reported to me there was a couple of players that was in town from New York. And they was sniffing around one his girls and mine. My territory was from The Flame Night Club on 16th and Nicollet Avenue South in Minneapolis to the White Castle Hamburger joint on Lake Street and Blaisdell Avenue South.

When I caught up with my lady, she told me it was just conversation that she had with the out of town players. I took the money my lady handed me, and for all the players to see I tore the money up into little pieces and threw the money in her face, right there in front of The Flame Night Club. I told her, "You know the rules of the game! I will deal with you later." The word got out on the streets real, quick that I was not the player to be played with cause I tear up money!

And a player who plays gangster to protect what is his can't be wrapped too tight. Hanging people from balconies was threatening but not crazy. Tearing up money that was crazy and unheard of. Because people NEED their money. And it left people to question if I would tear up her money what would, I do to her and anybody else who played with my money.

Also, during this time, a lot of players and their ladies was putting in overtime on the streets. Reason being was because two Hollywood black movie stars and a Minneapolis night club owner, was going to be sponsoring a two-day event called The Players Ball. The winner would get a two-week trip to Hollywood to be in an upcoming black movie that the two black movie stars was producing. The movie genre was: mack movie and/or black exploitation films that were big in the 1970's.

The players ball was going to be the first of its kind in Minneapolis, Minnesota. But other areas of the country were already doing them. The ball was pretty much going to imitate the 1973 movie *The Mack*. The players ball would include all the bells and whistles; people everywhere, everyone wearing their finest gear (clothing), drugs, alcohol, and beautiful women. All of the things that were displayed in the movie *The Mack*. Except one very, important thing most of the players who attended or participated in the players ball are real; not acting On the night of the players ball downtown Minneapolis blew up (had lots of excitement). The Othello Night Club had television news cameras, radio stations, model agencies, and newspaper writers all there for this big event. As I stepped-out the limousine on the first night of the players ball I wore a black pinstriped Italian suit, black and white Italian leather shoes, a white silk shirt, black silk tie, and a white Dobbs Godfather Hat. My gear (clothing) made my light skinned, 6'2" 200-pound frame feel and look like Hollywood material.

The news cameras and bright lights was shining on my outfit like it was gold. People was lined up on each side of the red carpet like I was a king going into the club to sit on my throne.

Yes! It was all eyes on me! The inside of the club was just as busy as the outside. Champagne, Dom Perignon was getting served at all the players' tables, waitresses was picking up three and four hundred-dollar tips. The ladies was dressed and looked so good. You could tell why God had chosen them to be queen of the universe. As The Player's Ball got under way, ten names were announced as the players' participants but only four of us got on the club stage.

It couldn't be just anyone, who could participate in the player's ball pageant. There were qualifications that had to be met. The qualifications was:

1.   Be able to provide your definition of what a player is.
2.   Have the lifestyle (be living the player lifestyle full-time).
3.   Have a street reputation
4.   Have street game knowledge
5.   Model (show off your player style), showboat
6.   Know and be able to share the player's rule book
7.   Have the ladies and money to back your game up

I made it through the first night as a runner up. I knew as well as the other three players in this competition that even though this players ball is not national come tomorrow night one of us will be the 1976 Player/Mack Of the Year in Minneapolis, Minnesota. The next afternoon in Downtown Minneapolis clothing stores, tailors and hat shops was full of players and hustlers getting their gear for tonight. I saw people I have never seen before in the shops. Hair salons and barber shops was full to the brim with men and women getting booted and suited for tonight's event.

I was having my special white satin Italian suit tailored at Kiefer's and would be picking up my red platform shoes at Brown's Clothing Store around 2p.m. My hair was already nice. Fried (hot combed/pressed), parted, and laying to the side. I ran into C.J. and Kenney coming out of Bob's Hat Shop. They told me they was on their way up the street to Market Barbecue to have some ribs for lunch. I told them if they wanted to ride with me first, so I could pick up my money from two of my ladies who was meeting me on Hennepin Avenue at Moby Dick's Club, lunch would be on me.

While at Moby's, we ordered drinks. I had a Tanqueray Gin while Kenney and C.J. had Courvoisier and Coke. It was good seeing Kenney. Him and C.J. was big time cocaine and heroin dealers. Kenney was pulling my coat (telling me) he knows there is a lot of money being bet on who would win the player's ball. The players ball judges was a couple of local celebrities, and one of them was from out of town. C.J. said a lot of their customers (people who bought drugs from them) was going to be there. I told Kenney I'm just going out to the ball to get high, dance, and to have fun.

I do know my wife, in-laws, my other ladies, family, and friends was glad I was chosen as a runner-up last night. But I had no intentions on winning. Even though I know my street game is tight. My lady's hot pants are fitting right and I just knew I had to keep on licking the honey so I could keep on tasting my money. Just as I was thinking to myself, two of my ladies approached the bar stool I was sitting on and handed me a wad of money.

Then Kenney came over to the bar stool I was sitting on. I stood up, we looked at each other as we gave one another the black hand-shake. With a smile Kenney said, "Play on player, play on. Yes, indeed." C.J. laughed out loud. The barbecue lunch sure is on you. We all started laughing as we walked out of the bar into the afternoon sun. My car pulled up so I could go home and get some rest before I went to the club. I needed to prepare myself for the big fight (The Player's Ball Event). My mental state was like any boxer knows you've got to come out ready to fight if you want to win. And I was playing to win.

One of my friend's said, "WOW! THIS IS THE REAL DEAL!" As the chauffeur opened the car door to my limo. As I got into my car I couldn't see nothing but Rolls Royce's, Mercedes Benz's, Cadillacs, Continentals, BMW's and Porsche's lined up on both sides of Hennepin Avenue as far as the eye could see. When me and the ladies got inside the club it was packed. Wall to wall with nothing but ladies of the night, and players. Three of the local television news stations was there with a lot of other security people.

There was so many camera light bulbs flashing that the inside the club looked as bright as daylight. I understand a little now what the Hollywood Oscar Awards must feel like. Cause there was definitely some actor wanna bee's at the players ball. The wanna bee's to me was the fake player's. The cats that might look the part, have on the gear, but in all realness they've never been on a real player's journey.

Master player Don Juan American Pimp would agree with me on this. As the player's contest got under way, the four of us runners-up took to the stage one last time to model our outfits and dance to a record of our choice. The song I chose was "Tear The Roof Off The Mother Sucker" by Parliament from the Mothership Connection Album. You can never go wrong when you choose the mothership connection to get the party started.

After a few more words from the radio station announcer from KUXL, it was time to announce what all the people at the Othello Night Club was waiting hear. Who won the %$#* contest! Who was going to be The Mack Of The Year? As two of the runner-ups left the stage, it was just T. and myself standing on the stage. In the hot, bright colored lights that hoovered over us, I could see everything in the club moving in slow motion. I was so high from the alcohol and cocaine that I just wanted to leave the stage with the other two runner-ups so I could ice up my nose with another hit of cocaine.

My Giorgio Armani white suit, red silk shirt, and white tie, only made the red rhinestone platform shoes, and my red Dobbs hat stand out. The shiny flashing lights hovering over me made my dazzling smile look even brighter. I was on, this evening. Nothing could shine brighter than I did in my outfit. As I was into my thoughts about how good I looked, my thoughts was interrupted as I saw a trophy being handed to the other guy as he was being led off the stage.

Then I heard, "THE MACK OF YEAR! THE MACK OF THE YEAR! THE MACK OF THE YEAR I was handed a trophy while camera lights were flashing, and media people hit me from all sides. The camera lights were so bright I almost couldn't see my wife and in-laws at the table in the crowd of onlookers. My ladies that worked for me was all over me! Yes! I stay true to the game! Yes! I was announced player of the year of Minnesota!

After the player's ball contest my celebrity status was boosted up in the game. Which meant more money for the ladies in my stable and myself. I was now no longer a pimp. I was a gentleman of leisure with money coming at me all the time. I also had to be careful of the player haters and their jealousy, as well as already being on law enforcement's hate list. Sadly, though when I went to visit my grandmother and great-grandmother. I told them a very, different story about the trophy. They saw me on T.V. several times but they thought I had won the player of the year contest for a basketball competition. They was so proud of me, I didn't have the heart to tell them what the trophy was really for.

My grandmother wanted to keep the trophy at her house on the fireplace mantel in the big white house they lived in on James Avenue in North Minneapolis. The trophy stayed at their house until they both (grandmother, great-grandmother) passed, away. It makes me sad, when I think about how proud they were to see the trophy and believe that it came from something like a basketball game. I get teary-eyed even as I am writing this. I never told my grandmothers the truth about the players ball. But I hope they hear me up in heaven and understand I just couldn't wipe that happy smile off their faces. So now I keep the trophy as a reminder of repentance.

Anyway, back to the story. Like I said everything was going well in the land of the players. I was a gentleman of leisure with several ladies of the night that were in the business of selling their sweet tasty products to the highest bidder. When the contests was over and the ladies and I got back to business I was waiting to go on my trip to Hollywood that I won as one of the prizes from the players ball. But I was on probation and told that if I leave the State of Minnesota while on bail, and do not come back from Hollywood in time to appear in court, there would be an arrest warrant issued.

I thought why am I paying for a private lawyer? I pay the cost to be the boss, my crime lifestyle is going well, and my attorney can't get even get me out of a warrant so I can leave for Hollywood. When I won the contest, I was not thinking about the forgery and theft case that I had got some time back. So now I'm waiting outside a courtroom in downtown Minneapolis with my $1000.00 suit my $400.00 Italian shoes waiting to be called into the courtroom. This judge stands between me and Hollywood. I was dressed to impress.

We were finally called into the court room. My lawyer begins to explain to the judge to let me off on probation because winning the players ball meant I could possibly be another Minnesota movie star, since the grand prize was a trip to Hollywood and an appearance in a movie. After my lawyer's argument, the court room went from silence to a very loud KABOOM from the gavel hitting the top of the judge's bench. The judge looked down at me and my lawyer from his bench with a laser-eyed glare and said in a strong, firm voice, "I am not condoning anyone in my court room for pimping! Five years!"

As the judge slammed down his gavel again, he said, "I will stay the original sentence if your client is willing to do six months in the workhouse. And he does not get into any more trouble. Pimping! You two get out of my court room."

I was very, upset as I looked at my lawyer. I agreed to the six months. But where's the justice! I'm missing out on Hollywood because this dude didn't argue my case so the judge would understand my position. I thought to myself.

This is no way to treat a gentleman like myself. With me going to the workhouse I had to forfeit my prize to Hollywood. One day you're a king and the next you're in the workhouse. Talk about being knocked off the throne. Wow! Workhouse/jail time again. I guess players can fall.

NOW YOU SEE TIME, NOW YOU DON'T PART I

But do not overlook this one fact, beloved, that with the
Lord one day is as a thousand years, and a thousand
years as one day

—2 Peter 3:8
English Standard Version (ESV)

Wow! I am so sick of looking at jail bars. How many times, and how much time is it going to take before I wake up to the fact that crime don't pay?! But truthfully, crime is all I know. So, how do I take what I've learned committing crime and apply those skills to legitimate work? Time seemed to be slipping by me. A change needs to be made; but how? And more importantly, when? And on top of those questions, what? What work could I do? What work am I qualified for? Where would I go to ask these questions? I don't even know what legitimate work options would suit my skills.

While I was getting use to my new accommodations at the Hennepin County Workhouse near Plymouth, Minnesota, the player of the year celebrity status I gained from winning the players ball was still fresh in the streets from the media that covered the event, those who attended the event, and those who heard about the event. So, inside the workhouse walls I was considered one of those players who got a chance to live the extravagant lifestyle people associated with a player from the movies.

So, there was still a lot of talk about it (the players ball and the life-style), while I was in the workhouse. Time was going forward. People were living their lives and yet for me, my life seemed; glamorous but I was not doing anything outside of the game, which is a never-ending hustle. When you work a regular job, you may get a break. But the hustle, street-life is 24/7.

Although the 24/7 can often make a day feel like a month. Even when you have down time you never know who you can trust or who you can depend on. Making down time more of a make sure you're on guard at all times, time.

Speaking of time flying by, here It was December of 1978 and I am having another baby girl. The second one by wife who was my main lady in the game. However, her being my main lady and pregnant did not stop me from cheating on her with the next-door neighbor. She was on her way to the army and did not know she was pregnant with my baby when she left. When they found out she was pregnant the army gave her a choice to keep the baby and get out with a medical discharge or have an abortion.

I loved her and wanted her to come home with my child. She had my baby a couple months later. I did believe I messed up her chance to get away from Minneapolis and experience something different, but I never said it out loud. By February of 1979 I had five children, a son and four daughters. I always made a promise to myself that when- ever I had children they was always going to know who their father was. I loved all my kids' mothers in my own way. I just could not stay true or faithful to any of them.

In the game with five kids by several different women and now a second wife who was my main lady in the game and she stayed true to the game; she gave it her all to make sure our money kept coming in. I went from just worrying about myself and making sure my ladies in the game were taking care of, to having others in my world and taking care of them (my kids) hinged on a promise I made to myself. That I would always take care of my kids and spend time with them.

A promise I worked hard at trying to keep even with my world spinning out of control all around me. Now a father of five by several other women and a wife. I was making a lot of runs back and forth to Chicago with a couple of drug dealer associates. I made the runs 'cause I would get a better deal on the product there (in Chicago) then I could in Minnesota. The money from the runs also allowed me to have my own personal stash (of drugs) that was not for sale.

And it's true what they say, a dealer should not be their own best customer. I became an addict and alcoholic. I lost all my ladies of the night. My wife and all the women I was cheating with. After what felt like losing everything, what really tore me down was when I found out that one of my girlfriends had committed suicide. She told her sister and family that she had a whole lot of love for me. She was already sick with sickle cell and her mental state was important to managing her disease.

Her sister told me she would cry to her about me not changing from my wicked ways. Her family was so upset with me they didn't even want me to come to the funeral. I wanted to go but out of respect for her family, I chose not to attend. It makes me sad when I think about her. I really liked, maybe even loved her but the street-life was more important to me at the time than one woman.

I remember when I would go see her. I use to pull my car right up under her second floor balcony at her apartment in North Minneapolis. I would climb up on her balcony and she would meet me at her balcony window with the most beautiful smile I have ever seen. Along with her committing suicide my life was a chaotic mess. It was also during this time that my brother got shot.

I went from snorting coke, to taking pills, I went from drinking Tanqueray Gin and Courvoisier liquor, to drinking Mad Dog 2020 and Wild Irish Rose Wine. I went from living in an extravagant apartment to sleeping under doorsteps. I had to ask my mom if I could crash at her and my stepdad's place for a while. I tore up my car because I was drunk and hit two parked cars and a stop sign. Oh, how the mighty have fallen. Believe me when I say these was some of the coldest days in my life.

I went from wearing $1000 suits and driving a nice silver Cadillac to bringing my clothes to my parent's house, in a garbage bag. I went from wearing Italian shoes to wearing broken down shoes. While staying with my parents I would borrow my brother's clothes and shoes just to keep up with what little pride and image that I had left.

1980 was just around the corner and me and my stepdad had got pretty close.

I also had a steady woman I was seeing. We had known and liked each other from back in the day when we used to hang out at the youth center over in South Minneapolis. When S-Ann and I reunited she shared with me where she had been and what she had been doing. She went into the military and came out a few years later.

She had two little kids, a boy and a girl. She had a nice place and a good job. We moved in together and things was going ok with us. I had got a little cleaning job, stopped taking pills and the only crime I was doing was using a few different names for different reasons. S-Ann was faithful to me, but I wasn't faithful to her. And once I started cheating, my drinking became heavier and heavier. One day I was coming home from staying out all night and saw a bunch of people standing in front of our building. They looked like they was pulling and grabbing on different stuff.

I asked someone what was going on. He said there was a lot of nice clothes falling from the sky. And as I got closer, I could see what the commotion was all about. I looked up at the building and S-Ann was standing on 13th floor balcony. Her hands were letting my clothes float down from the sky. My pants and shirts were tied together by shoe-strings from my shoes. The clothes were floating from the apartment balcony to the ground looking like a parachute as they slowly floated and drifted to the ground.

S-Ann was yelling down at me, "YOU LIKE TO STAY OUT ALL NIGHT JUMPING IN WOMENS' BEDS! YOUR SO BAD JUMP UP HERE AND GET ME!" After the people on the street under the balcony saw and heard what was going on, the guys let go of my clothes thinking they might be jinxed. I said, "Honey! I beg of you to give me one more chance! It's time for me to go into treatment."

I thought to myself, okay I am Lord! I am here, I am sick and tired of being sick and tired. So, fix me. Can we make a deal Lord? I am going to give you 85 percent of me, maybe even ninety. If you just fix me! I was on my way to a treatment program. What I would find out is, it's true what they say about treatment programs; it will work for you, if you are willing to do the work.

I felt with God in my program I would do pretty-good. And I did. I was getting clean after many years of using drugs and drinking. S-Ann and I was still together. I was sober. I was living in a nice house. I had a nice car. And I was now working a nice job as a drug counselor. I was seeing my kids regularly along with having another baby on the way by S-Ann. So here it was 1983 and I thought this is the way God wanted me to be living. Just as I was getting comfortable with my new life, I was about to be thrown a curve ball that felt more like a sucker punch.

I was the DJ (disc jockey) for a weekend youth function when I got a call around 12 midnight. The person on the other end of the phone said that my great grandmother was dying. She was taken to the hospital right across the street from where the youth function was being held. I was the first one to get up to my great grandmother's hospital room. Once I got to her room I could tell MaMa (great grandmother) was on her way to meet with the Lord. I saw her pass- away.

I took my great grandmother's death very, hard. During this time, I had a white friend named Steve. And wherever he's at I want to thank him from the bottom of my heart. Because he hung with me through some really hard times. Steve and I worked as recovery counselors together. He was a very, good friend and helped me work through the grief of losing my grandmother. S-Ann and I named our sixth child after my great-grandmother, Carrie. After the events of 1983, 1984 was a very-long year. During this time, it seemed as though time moved really, slow.

I was still a youth drug counselor, but still respected in the streets. I knew this cause when I would see my home boys I ran with or did jail time with we were still boys for life. I felt if God was not judging me and he (God) was changing me, then He (God) would do the same for them. But was I really changing? Or was I just going through the motions because working a job and having a family was the American way. And I did tell God I would give Him 85% of me. Maybe that's why change isn't actually feeling comfortable. I'm only in it half-heartedly.

I began to spend a lot more time with my grandmother. It was her mother who died, and she missed her mom deeply. I would take my grandmother to the places she needed to go, and we would talk a lot. She seemed to be so sad. I think it was because after her mom (my great grandmother) died, my grandmother was living alone, without my great grandmother. It was still 1984 and I was still the DJ at the youth place across the street from the hospital where my great grandmother had died.

As I was playing music at the youth club and thinking about my great grandmother my thoughts was interrupted by someone coming up to the DJ booth at almost 12 midnight. The person told me they just got a call from the hospital across the street and that I needed to get over there right away! I thought to myself, now my grandmother was slipping away. Why God? When I got to the hospital even before I saw my grandmother I was crying and sobbing, tears for her not to leave me!

"Where was God at? And why is He taking my grandmother?", I asked myself. My grandmother said to me, I would be ok. I said, "But I still owe you $25 that you let me have for couple of music albums. You got to stay so I can pay you back." She just smiled at me and said, "Lee God has you. You will be okay." The nurse told me to call and see was my mom and ask if the family was on their way. When my mom, stepdad and my friend Steve was coming down the hall I had to tell them that grandmother went home to the Lord.

I told my mom that she was smiling so I know her and Big MaMa is together. To this day I wonder and I sometimes cry, when I think about; how was it that great grandmother and grandmother died at the same time? Right after midnight. And how was it that they died in the same month, although one year apart. And how was it that I was the DJ at the youth club close to the hospital on those same nights? When my great grandmother and my grandmother died, did God's timing put me there at the same time, twice in the same place for a reason?!

Playing my music in Elliot Park, right across from Methodist Hospital, next to the Bethlehem Christian College was not just a job, it was a blessing. At the time my grandparents died I did not know fourteen years later I would be directing a women's support group and I would be doing public speaking about alcohol and drug addiction recovery in the same places. I often thought back to what my grandmother told me. "Lee you're going to be okay."

It's during these speaking engagements that I felt, and I continue to feel my grandparents' presence. When I started on my speaking engagement journey I began yelling, "WAKE-UP" to my brothers and sisters who were attending the recovery speaking engagements. I would yell "WAKE-UP!!!" to the attendees hoping, praying they would hear the call and take their life back, drug-free.

NOW YOU SEE TIME, NOW YOU DON'T PART II

The Lord is not slow to fulfill his promise as some count slowness, but is patient toward you, not wishing that any should perish, but that all should reach repentance.

—2 Peter 3:9
English Standard Version (ESV)

YES, 1984 WAS a very sad year. I stayed working as a drug counselor until about 1987. It was also in 1987 that I had a relapse (returned to drinking alcohol and using drugs). And even though I know my relapse was mostly from the grief of losing my grandparents, I quit my job because it wasn't right to speak on or about recovery while using. I did not want to be a hypocrite on top of being depressed and grieving.

I was also on a very thin line with boundary issues. I knew I couldn't talk about recovery and be getting high. I was hurting and in a lot pain about my life. At this time, I also wished I knew who my dad was. It would hurt me when I saw people on TV getting reunited with their lost mom or dad. I just wanted to know what was my, dad like. Did my dad even know I existed? Do I look like him? Talk like him? Act like him?

It's funny how societal and organizational systems work. I had all the support in the world when I decided I was going to put myself in recovery. I was embraced by those in recovery and the recovery field. But I was also never forgotten or treated badly by the people I knew from the streets. Both groups knew I was trying to do right. But when my grandparents passed-away I relapsed. My grandparents were my rock. I could always count on their love, wisdom, and support. It was unwavering, nurturing, and always there. So, when I relapsed it was their love, nurturing, support, and wisdom that I missed and needed.

When I relapsed the recovery-community walked away from me. What's interesting about the recovery community walking away from me is oftentimes those who go through recovery are told to take it one day at a time. Recovery participants are also told we will be with you throughout your recovery. Well, recovery does not have a timeline. You are always recovering. You are just in different stages of the process. From the first day you start until you die, you will always be tempted. So, when the recovery community walked away from me but the people, I knew from the streets were still in my corner I was angry, confused, and hurt.

The recovery community did not give me support at all when I asked for help. Every one of my fellow treatment counselors and some friends who knew they know I was struggling walked away. I felt they walked away from a young black man that was in need, of their help. Isn't mental health assistance and recovery about helping you when you stumble? Them walking away or turning their backs on me during my relapse meant for them recovery was all about the money and their organization's image, not the people recovering.

It was the gangs, the thugs, the hustlers, the players, and the ladies of the night that welcomed me back into the street life with open arms. I was told by one of my street associates "Lee even though you was working for the system now, you never turned your back on your people. When you saw one of us hurting or we thought you didn't trust us anymore, you showed us we could trust you. And in return we showed you that you could trust us. Lee your word was your bond. We remember when our kids would act up and skip school, no matter what time it was you would come into the projects over in North Minneapolis, track them down and take them back to group or school." The black community when I was growing up believed in the community as a village motto and it was those in the street life that often reminded me of that. No matter what was going on in the streets the community still cared about their children.

I now had custody of my son and I thought by moving out in the suburbs of Burnsville, Minnesota with my sister and her daughter I would be able to keep my son out of harm's way, even though I was now back in the streets. I had one foot in the street game and another foot outside the game. I always remembered I still had my boy to raise, but I was back in a place where I had to rebuild what I had lost and the street game was the only way I knew to get that done quickly.

I was spending time with some of my kids, but it was really depending on what kind of mood their moms would be in. If we weren't arguing or we weren't fighting over something they wanted me to buy or give them money that I didn't have when they asked or that I couldn't buy when they asked, I could usually get the kids. And child support was always an issue because work during this time was not steady.

Now, my physical environment did not match the life I was living. Living out in the suburbs was always nice. You could tell how other people lived compared to the inner city. The streets and sidewalks were so clean they looked like the neighborhoods in movies and T.V. shows. You would not even see a candy wrapper on the pavement. I thought being out here would keep my son away from the temptation of the streets. But my son started getting into trouble.

My son got sent up to a state boy's home for a while. Even though I was still out in the streets I never thought he would begin to follow in my footsteps. Maybe I never saw it coming because my own childhood and teenage years were disruptive and far from normal. So, I never considered a child would do what they see you do. I did not have the knowledge to take that into consideration. And even though my son never actually saw me actively participate in street life activities it does not mean that he may not have seen things around the house or heard from others about what I had done and was doing.

I felt bad and sad for my son cause I know where street life can lead. I know the ups, the downs, and the pitfalls of the game. But also, he was still my son and I wished he didn't go down that road. But how do you stop it? Now, it was going into the ninety's and I was pretty much back in the game with one of my family members. He was a big-time drug dealer and he allowed me, to be cut in on the action. I also had a woman from Japan. She was a top banker's daughter who worked in a law firm. And I had a woman from Trinidad. With these classy ladies on my arms I was introduced to more of the white-collar crimes and lifestyle.

These women could work magic with computers, pen, and paper. They knew how to emboss (stamp a design into paper)—make fake money and transfer that fake money into credible business establishments. Now I went from playing street games, to becoming a hustler in the white-collar crime game. I was moving up fast in a world I thought was too slow for me. I was living large once again. Only this time the building I was living in had a racquetball court, a tennis court, and swimming pools (yes more than one), a yellow Cadillac, a champagne-colored Riviera, and a white Lincoln Continental.

Just to keep low key (unnoticed) when I was in the city, I use to have my brother Melvin pick my oldest daughters and step kids up and I would let them just hang-out in the luxurious sunken living room apartment. I also let them play and swim in the indoor pool. I would shower the kids with gifts that I brought back from my Las Vegas drug runs. My cousin Mick and his women also moved into the apartment building I was living in. Cousin Mick, his women, and my family members who were part of the business, all lived the lavish lifestyle. We'd party all night well into the day.

With the family drug business doing well and my money right again I saw and knew that people could only wish for and dream about the life I had. The business made me see how easy it was for a person to turn criminal. Especially, if you have been down that road before. I have tasted the devil's temptations and I am now back for more. And now that I'm back in the game the devil quickly began replacing the quiet life I had with bitter sweet worldly possessions. But the worldly possessions and fast money were not free. Everything came with anger, hate, treachery, and deceitfulness; lack of morals included. All of it was right back in my tasteless mouth. But maybe, this is what giving God 85% gets you.

I thought making a deal with God would help me through this relapse, but it didn't. Where was He (God) at when I fell? Where was He at when MaMa (great grandmother) died? Where was He at when grandmother died? Why didn't He help grandmother with the loneliness she felt missing her mother, were the thoughts and questions I had for God. After all, I even gave God 85% of myself. Didn't he know I was here? I probably would of gave Him 90% if He didn't take my grandparents away.

God knew the women in our family along with my great grandmother and grandmother were the rocks that held everything together. How could He (God) take them? The men in the family had it together, or so I thought, providing for our family network, but it was the women from far back as I can remember that made the sacrifices for their children.

Speaking for myself the only thing I did to young women was use them. I would take what was given to me and use their love selfishly with no respect for their feelings or gentle emotions. The only thing women was going to get back from me was a bunch of words and riddles of fake integrity. But I wouldn't know this about myself until years later, when I would be taking my own personal inventory in recovery.

It was women like my grandmothers who upheld the household, how to behave (table manners, how to speak to an adult) and family traditions. MaMa and grandmother would not let us kids play or eat in the living room, we prayed as a family at dinner, we were not allowed to bring our family disagreements, we always got together for the holidays, we could speak to our grandmothers about our other siblings but they would never speak a mean word about any of us. We just knew they would want us to resolve the disagreement and remember all we had was one another.

Once MaMa (great grandmother) and grandmother passed away, it felt like all our family traditions died along with them. And maybe that's why they would make sure we always got together for the holidays because they wanted us to continue the tradition when they were no longer here. Even though my brother and sister attempted to keep the family together and uphold the values and traditions, something was still missing. During holidays we didn't get together for holiday dinners anymore. Everyone seemed to be off doing his or her own thing.

Like watching the game on T.V. at their house or talking on the phone if they did come to the house for holiday dinner. The sense of family unity didn't just seem to be missing, it was missing.

The problem of family traditions being lost when Big MaMa passes, or grandma leaves us due to dying is still a problem today. Our elders held us together and we did not respect what they were doing. It's our lack of family unity that has spilled out into the streets with people looking for, wanting, needing someone to care for them and about them. My grandmothers gave me genuine love. My mom didn't understand me. But how could she, she was 14 years old when she had me. She was more of a sister than a mother. Not complaining just expressing why our relationship was such a tense one.

MaMa and grandmother were the buffers between the two of us. And whoever my father was, I hated him cause I could not see the mirror of me. Who am I? Do I walk like him? Do I talk like him? Do I have his personality? Is he humorous? I have questions God! Where are you at? God where is my fatherly mirror. The mirror that allows people to say you look just like your dad and I could look at him and smile. The mirror that shows me I want my son to be just like me and my dad. The mirror that says I'm special because My Dad, stayed. I hurt so much inside.

Do l want to kill someone? Do I want to kill myself? I think not! I Will Make My Own Fatherly Mirror! So, MY CHILDREN NEVER HAVE TO FEEL THE PAIN I FEEL BECAUSE MY MIRROR DID NOT THINK I WAS IMPORTANT ENOUGH TO STAY. GOD, I DON'T KNOW IF YOU HEAR ME OR NOT! BUT THANK YOU FOR MY CHILDREN, AND THEIR MOTHERS. THANK YOU FOR YOUR GRACE.

WHEN THE STREETS
NO LONGER SPEAK

The Lord is near to the brokenhearted and saves the crushed in spirit.

—Psalm 34:18

He heals the brokenhearted and binds up their wounds.

—Psalm 147:3
English Standard Version (ESV)

TIME WAS MOVING by so fast and it seemed like the years of my life were being spent so quickly. Here it was already 1991 and the world events in the news were of no interest to me. Events that included Iraq invading Kuwait, Rodney King getting brutally beat by cops which was captured on videotape, Mikhail Gorbachev resigns as president of the Soviet Union, Gulf War: An Iraqi scud missile hits an American military barracks in Dhahran, Saudi Arabia killing 28 United States Army Reserve e.g U.S. Army Reservists from Pennsylvania, and the first Gulf War ends; just to name a few historical highlights of 1991.

Except what was happening with troubled youths hurting and killing each other meant more to me than worldly events. For some reason I could identify with them (troubled youths) and I could sense there was a lot of pain weaving its way through their hearts and coming out in ways that often harmed themselves and others. Pain that I'm sure they thought they w ere keeping hidden by gathering with others of the same mentality, the same struggles, the same life goal of getting them before they get you. Pain they believed they kept locked away in their young minds. Pain they did not understand came out through daily actions of minor and major aggressions.

I often wonder if their self-conscious provides them a glimpse into what a walking, talking emotional time bomb looks like. Not seeing a way out, but possibly believing someone may offer a glimpse of light to break down the walls of anger that have built up over so many young years. Years where crime began at 11 years of age due to the circumstances you are born into. How does one soften or penetrate a hardened heart that has rarely seen kindness, goodness, and genuine acts of unconditional help?

I was that youth with the explosive attitude. That saw the world as transactional. Everyone owed me something. And those who couldn't pay must be harmed. Harm meant whatever I thought should happen to someone in that moment. Eventually, I began to understand in reality it wasn't the world, it was the system that I was born into. A system that gave me a sneak preview of the black and white systemic as well as contextual equality of being born black, male, and into a family that saw self-preservation of self as commandment number one.

My life has seemed to be a series of movie clips. Clips that moved me from crime to crime, moments of what would seem to some as living high (literally and figuratively); with women, cars, luxury apartments, money, travel, trips, clothes, guns, fights, jail, and prison. Often, encouraged by family to keep the show going. Being introduced to such a lifestyle at a very, young age how would I ever discern right from wrong or good from bad? In other words, develop a conscious. That was the questions that kept running through my mind.

And if the question of discerning right from wrong was running through my mind it meant that I did have a soul. It meant my spirit was trying to break through the cement the world had built around my soul. It meant that I was going to have to figure out what living outside of this lifestyle I have known all my life would look like for me. But the answer for moving forward with a new lifestyle did not come swiftly. Nor, did it come without the temptation of being pulled back.

My cousin and some of my family was still in the street game. And even though we lived in the suburbs we still did a lot of drug dealing and partying in Minneapolis and Saint Paul, MN. I was still raising some of my kids and taking care of some of my kids and steps kids. Meaning some lived with me and some didn't. But I would pick them up, take them out to eat, buy them the things they needed and did my best to be there for them.

By no means was I a perfect father, I just did the best I could under the circumstances. Several women and even more kids, but I was determined to be a dad. Although being there for them often seemed like gathering the United Nations together to discuss world peace. An allday project where little gets accomplished. My cousin Mick and I were cool. He understood what I was dealing with. Even though I was still living somewhat of the rich life due to the street game.

With other women still in my life I fell in love with a women I met over in Saint Paul. She reminded me of a woman I had feelings for back in the day. Back when my brother would come over for dinner. It's funny when I think about it because now, my brother is sitting here packaging up his cocaine to sell. One day my brother left about $2,000 of powdered cocaine on a plate that still needed to be packaged at my apartment.

While me and brother was out on a run my lady friend who had a key to my place came over. She cooked us some fried chicken the night before. She told me she would be back the next day to clean up the house. When she came back and saw plates on the table she thought it was cooking flour and washed the plate that had the unpackaged cocaine on it with the rest of the dishes. When we got back to the apartment and saw what happened my brother was so upset.

He said, "If I see her on the street, I'm going to beat up her on sight! Then beat her up again in my sleep!" I told him that he should have put the rest of the drugs up with his weight scale. Needless to say, even after giving the $2,000 back to my brother he still did not let what she did go. Although he never hurt her. I told him my friend did not do any kind of drugs and she did not live that lifestyle. I still could not get my brother to come over to another dinner at my place.

He told me he if he gets hungry, he would, hold up a Kentucky Fried Chicken restaurant and eat where he knows his drugs wouldn't get wash down the drain by a square crazy lady. The woman I met over in Saint Paul just took my breath away the moment I met her. She had long black hair, and eyes that could see right through you in a beautiful way. Her golden-brown slim body made her desirable to any man that crossed her path.

The only problem was she was a drug addict. But how could a drug dealer like myself pay attention to such a minor detail. My cousin was telling me I was a fool in love. It was few months away from the new year, in love again, but I believed she was in love with me too. On October 31 1991, Halloween Night, the biggest snowstorm Minnesota had seen in years blew snow and wind across city, suburban, and rural streets. This storm brought all activities in the State of Minnesota to a grinding halt. Minnesota where people ski on snow, sled on snow, snowshoe on snow came to a full stop.

The streets were no longer speaking! Some people called this Halloween storm, the perfect storm. The snowfall affected everyone in the state. And if you were outside in the snowstorm either on foot or in your vehicle, you were in for a rude awakening if you thought you were going someplace. Or you thought you were going to get back from somewhere.

I was glad when winter came and went. In April of 1992, S.E. became pregnant with my seventh child. She agreed to go into treatment where she stayed as long as I agreed to be supportive of her and be there when she came home from treatment. I agreed and kept drug dealings away from her. She kept her word and stayed in treatment. S.E. gave birth to a heathy baby girl. And after that she was gone. She gave my daughter to me to raise and said she was sorry. But the drugs was too strong. The hold they had on her would not allow her to walk away. She knew she was struggling.

S.E. told me that she wanted to keep her promise to me, and that she loved me and my other kids that was living with me at the time but couldn't. Then she was gone back to the drug infested streets. Street-life had its ups and downs. This is a time when there started to be more downs then ups. My oldest daughter was taking care of her mom who had severe injuries that came from an abusive relationship. The guy almost killed her (my child's mom).

My son and one of my daughters were sent up to a boy's home and girl's home. I thought my second oldest daughter, being put in a girl's home as teen would stop her from going down the wrong path. But as life would have it, the family bloodline created another little bad gangster. My third daughter who was 12 years old at the time helped me take care of her three-week-old baby sister. My cousin Mick and I was still running the streets. But now I had to figure out how to slow down. Because I was taking care of kids, which was more of a stress then I thought it would be.

I use to think to myself as a good father. I take my hat off to all the single mothers in the world. I didn't realize all they went through taking care of children until I had that responsibility. On one sunny day while me and my cousin was sitting on a big rock in this suburb park, drinking a big bottle of beer (a forty), Mick suddenly had this very serious look of unbelief in his eyes. He looked at me and started speaking. He said, "Lee we been on a lot of road and air trips together, but I am going on a trip to Hawaii, Maul, with my girl M. 'cause it will be the last trip I will be taking. Because after I get back cousin I will be going on my next trip alone. And no one can come with me. So cousin I need you to do me a big favor, look out after my girl for me."

Mick and I had ran the streets together for a good while now, and we had big fun! But I was not sure where this conversation was coming from or where it was going. I asked my cousin, "Can you do me a favor and we hang out in the streets just a little while longer?" Mick said, "Lee I am going blind. And you see man there's no other way I can tell you this, but I got only a few months left man. Cause I am dying!"

I know we were both high off the weed and beer, and I knew Mick used cocaine, so I thought this a con, for me to give him some of my product (cocaine) on credit. My thought was interrupted by Mick speaking to me again in a crackling whisper. It seemed like he was trying to hold back tears. He said, "Remember Lee, me telling you some time back when I was in the Navy and I got shot. And they had gave me a blood transfusion?" I nodded yes. "Well come to find out the blood the Navy gave me from the blood transfusion was contaminated with the auto immune deficiency syndrome (AIDS) virus. That's what I've been going to court about all this time. I finally won my case. That's why me and M. had been taking those trips together with you and your lady friends. I wanted to live it up and party before I left this planet."

I begin believing what Mick was telling me. I knew about AIDS. I knew it was just as deadly as cancer. But I never knew the disease would hit my cousin like it did. I never thought about the last journey a man travels as he prepares to die. The last streets we would walk together, the last moments of time we spent together would stay with me for the rest of my life. Mick wasn't lying about going blind. M. or I would take him where he needed to go (doctor's appointments and other business-related errands).

And once again it seemed like the world was moving so fast I couldn't catch up. Cause right be for my eyes, in a matter of weeks, not months; I saw my healthy active young cousin who loved to dance and party at some of the best hotel suites in the country with his strong 5'7" slim body now was deteriorating right be for my eyes. In a matter of days, I had to carry him from the car to house. Mick could not run the streets anymore. He lost so much weight he was looking more like a brown skeleton.

He would be in so much pain, that when people came over to see him and would be talking to him, the slightest whispers or noise would give Mick excruciating pain. I could imagine how hard it was on M. who lived with him. We would take turns caring for him. While she was at work I would come down to his house and watch him. Sometimes I could get a light laugh out of him. Especially when he would ask me to give him some more cocaine on credit because the morphine he was prescribed had worn off and he would be back in pain.

I would then say, "Fool your dying! How you going to pay me back! Don't' think I won't get you out the coffin so you can pay me first." He chuckled! His girl did not like me giving Mick the drugs. But when he would sadly look at her and she saw the pain in his eyes, she didn't object to Mick getting high. It was hard for me to see Mick and I go from eating steaks together, to giving him baby food, or mixing something up real fine so that he could at least taste it.

On Mick's last day I asked him did he talk to God? Did he pray? I don't know why I asked him that. I don't think we really ever talked about God. Mick's eyes was wide open and even though he could not see anything, he whispered, "I will be ok." As Mick's last days on earth were coming to an end, I would like to believe that him and God did talk to each other. And what he meant was God said he would be ok.

I'll never forget Mick and I sitting on that big rock out in Burns-ville, MN like it was our own sanctuary having a chat about his sit-uation. I looked at Mick one last time before the doctors and nurses covered his face and head up with the white sheet. There's no return from the white sheet being pulled over your head. I felt Mick got a raw deal. Fighting for his country, only to be honored with carrying something back home that there was no cure for. My Spirit was full of sadness as I walked around the lonely suburban streets.

These streets were not like city streets. They were quiet and silent. Almost a scary quiet. My cousin and I were used to the city streets that seemed alive and adventurous, and even though some of the streets could be dangerous, to Mick and me the city streets spoke another language. A language that only people like Mick and me could hear. And even with sidewalks that provide cracks of knowledge you still have to understand the tone of the streets.

A tone that could only be heard when someone dies in your arms and the streets cannot explain or speak that life away with reason that comforts or alleviates the pain. I often wonder if the streets my cousin was up against in the war, was a black and white thing (hate of skin color) or a contextual thing (hate of the way a person thinks or believes). Or was there a silent gray hate that had not yet appeared to me because things in my world are so concrete. Gray is too confusing it provides too many layers of reasons for hate, love, anger. I want to see a street that no longer speaks. I want to see a street that provides true peace and true calmness to give my heart some reconciliation.

THE MAN WITHOUT A COMMUNITY THE COMMUNITY WITHOUT THE MAN

What shall we say then? Are we to continue in sin that grace may abound? By no means! How can we who died to sin still live in it?

—Romans 6:1–2

Be sober-minded; be watchful. Your adversary the devil prowls around like a roaring lion, seeking someone to devour. Resist him, firm in your faith, knowing that the same kinds of suffering are being experienced by your brotherhood throughout the world.

—1 Peter 5:8–9
English Standard Version (ESV)

MY COUSIN'S DEATH had a big impact on my life, I started to focus more on my children and family. I moved from the City of Burnsville to the suburbs of Eagan Minnesota with the help of my brother, M. I was still going back and forth to the north Minneapolis. Only this time it was to do good things for the youth and people of color. I opened a center called the V Center. And even though I wasn't doing drug counseling at this time, I came up with this idea with the help of people of the night (hustlers, players, gangsters, thugs, drugs dealers, and several professional athletes). I knew their small donations could help a lot of kids with getting books about their (Black) history, a half basketball court, art supplies, encouraging community members to volunteer and helping parents with money for food and baby diapers, old people could come up to the center and get money for their medicine.

People who came to the center did not have to fill out any paperwork because we gave them cash from our own resources. All people who wanted some form of cash assistance had to do was put down their name and take a book with them that my brother M. was giving out for free. Gangs were welcomed. They mentored and participated in activities that encouraged youth to look at different alternatives to gangs. All gang affiliated folk knew the V Center was neutral ground.

Several community organizations knew what we were doing and thought we were doing a good thing for the community. And we did it by pooling community resources together. Political leaders often had problems with what we were doing because not only did we pool community resources we didn't need help from any federal programs to offer people what they needed. I believe there was a lot of envy from the City of Minneapolis political establishment because the people of the night found a way to work around the system that often did nothing to help us anyway.

It's a system that I had been in and out of for a long time. And I always saw it as a system that was set up for people to fail. So, how could I continue to put my life and the life of my community members in the hands of a system way too comfortable with locking people up, paroling them with no assistance to succeed, offering a hand down and then blaming the person for failing. I personally knew of or was involved with six organizations in the State of Minnesota that in my opinion were created to keep their employees in middle class jobs. Not help the people the organizations were created to help.

Since my cousin's death I had a new passion beyond myself. I NEEDED to help people of color. And not just surface help. I NEEDED to know the help I was offering made a difference and a change in people's lives. Where the people came from and where their money came from did not matter. Why, because oftentimes they know life is difficult and can bring tough times to people who may have been born into circumstances beyond their control. But it does not mean they do not want to helped others. Sometimes it just means they haven't been asked. It also doesn't mean all street people are angels, but it does mean they deserve a chance to make a change or to help if they so choose.

Some of my people (who helped with the V Center), who I will call the people of the people of the night came from homelessness, criminal lifestyles, addiction, and unfortunate life circumstances which often introduced them to the game. People that helped the V Center came from all walks of life. No one was too good or too bad to help the youth, the community, the elderly. The people who helped the V Center knew the system was just as bad as the streets. It's just one claimed to be legally helping.

I took my family and moved from Burnsville, Minnesota to Eagan Minnesota. Both suburbs where Minnesota professional sports teams often moved their players. Even though I still lived in the suburbs, crime was finding a new home. It was becoming more prominent in the suburbs of Eagan. I don't know why I thought moving here would remove crime from my surroundings. I got caught up in what many people do 'nothing like that-crime-ever happens out here).

I felt betrayed and I felt lost! How could crime come out here? Why would crime come out here? I felt broken! Like a man without a community. I sometimes wondered how my life would have turned out if I had still been out there protesting back in 1967 against a system that still isn't right to this day. Here it was April of 1993, and I started seeing things going on out here in the suburbs like I saw in the city.

One day, I was looking out my apartment house window waiting for my 14-year-old daughter's school bus to drop her off at home, when I saw another school bus pull up the street and came to a complete stop. Three kids got off the bus and two of them started beating up on this other kid. They were stomping this kid bad. The real bad thing about it was there was a car passing by the parked school bus, but no one got out to help the kid who was getting beat up. People just drove past looking.

I could see from my apartment window the bus stop incident was starting to get more serious as I saw one of the kids going into his pocket. I ran down my steps without thinking. I just wanted to get down the steps and stop that kid from doing something that would affect the rest of his life. Once I got outside, I said to the kid who had his hand in his pocket, "Boy don't make the mistake I did. Whatever is in your pocket, and you use it, there is no turning back. Just walk away and get back on the bus with your friend."

The boy looked at me with cold eyes. I knew that look. I've seen that look so many times in my life. Especially when I looked in the mirror. The boy looked at me and then turned to his friend who was also listening. They both nodded their heads and got back on the bus. I helped the kid up just as the police pulled up. They asked me what I saw. I told them there were some kids fighting, I don't know if they were big or tall, short or small, black, blue, brown or white All I know is this kid was getting beat up. The police was talking to some other people in the apartment complexes as the school bus left the scene.

The nineties had not only brought in a new flavor of hip hop! But it also brought in a new flavor of gang activity and crime as well.

Racial profiling was also at an all-time high. I remember I was coming out of a McDonald's one day and because I asked a white lady why she was staring at me so, hard she had called the police because I looked suspicious while eating a hamburger. I was tackled to the ground, and tased by the Saint Paul Police several times and taken to jail for disorderly conduct.

But I also remember being pulled over on Lynch Road in Eagan, MN. This police officer had every right to arrest me and even take me to jail. But he didn't. He gave me a short lecture and let me go with a warning. I've seen good cops and bad cops and I was thinking about what just happened to me as I was pulled over in Eagan with these three kids in the car and I thought maybe I could bring some type of community programming to Eagan.

I had noticed even with my kids being out here in the suburbs, in this huge apartment complex we lived in, there was nothing for the one-hundred eighty kids of color to do. No community programming. I took it upon myself to talk with some of the other parents in the complex and after several conversations I created the Westcott Community Service Patrol. I took my vision a step further and founded an outdoor recreation center with a small basketball court and a day care center. Dakota County did their part by providing early childhood and family education services.

Dakota County School District and the Chief of Police got his department involved with our community programs as well. Our volunteers received a $50,000 grant and a temporary trailer house for Westcott, to be able to offer arts and crafts, and a youth job training program. I began to feel like me and my family belonged in this community. This was a big accomplishment for me.

Even though the city and local newspapers were talking about my past, I was focused on the present. I knew I would make a great park and youth director. And the community wanted me to run for youth city council. I was honored. I told myself I was never going to move back in the city of Minneapolis. Things were going well. And with the help of my life-long friend and brother M., families that lived in the complex and community volunteers I knew my life was changing for the better.

Former gang member helping clean up a suburban 'hood'

Ed Roy wasn't always a caring and considerate person. In fact, he used to be downright mean and nasty. A real hoodlum.

Roy, who's now 38, spent much of the first nine years of his life in Detroit before his mother moved the family back to north Minneapolis, where he was born. Without a father in the home and little money in his pockets, Roy said it was the street gangs — both in Detroit and Minneapolis — that provided him with male role models, albeit bad ones, and

After witnessing that incident, Roy decided he was going to do something to help his neighborhood before it was too late. Roy, along with the help of his town friend and Melvin

..., 39, had seen it all before in his long-ago lifetime as a pistol-packing gangster in north Minneapolis. Now, however, he and group of fellow ...'t residents are fighting the inner-city-style problems of his adopted second-ring suburban neighborhood with some inner-city-style solu-

Patrols continued on page 5B

ED ROY

territory was an accomplishment.

"You had that good feeling when you were riding around

Caddies, and you had that respect."

By all accounts, Roy was an accomplished gang member. As a ... ...ments.

It's been years since Ed Roy roamed the streets of Minneapolis as a member of the gang, but he carries memories that will haunt him forever. "You live with things," he said.

"Seeing your friends getting killed in front of you. I've seen people do things to other people and you live with it every day of your life."

Roy is trying to do what he ca... to make sure that kids in his ne... ...borhood don't have to liv... with those same kind of dark memories. He will never be ab... to erase the many negatives o... past, nor should he be totally forgiven for what he has done...

But real life was also close by as I was getting behind on rent. I told the landlord I would catch up. But I was not in the street game any more so money was hard to come by. Some political people from the community approached me and said because of my criminal background they didn't want my image put out there as being park director of their fine city. So, they hired a professional athlete to take the position I had created.

I was literally removed from the organization I created. I wasn't even offered a position picking up trash. My volunteers were offered positions but said they were not going to take the jobs they were offered because the community program was my dream and they wanted to help me with it. I told my volunteers they had families to feed. I told them to take the jobs and keep the dream alive for all the kids that will play in the park, run on court, utilize the programs offered, and for all the little ones that will be in the daycare center learning.

I shared with the volunteers, me and my kids will be ok. I told them that, but the truth of the matter was I was not ok. Again, I felt like I was failed by the system for trying to do right in my life. Again, I felt all alone. Here's another community that don't want me. Here's another community that I don't belong to. It's a feeling that crossed over into relationships as well.

A WORK IN PROGRESS
OR A PROGRESS
AT WORK

Therefore, my beloved, as you have always obeyed, so now, not only as in my presence but much more in my absence, work out your own salvation with fear and trembling, for it is God who works in you, both to will and to work for his good pleasure.

—Philippians 2:12–13

that I may know him and the power of his resurrection, and may share his sufferings, becoming like him in his death, that by any means possible I may attain the resurrection from the dead.

—Philippians 3:10–11

EVEN THOUGH MY love relationships were not up to par, being a single parent had its joy and Kodak (memorable) moments, as well as challenging ones. I was also becoming more powerful in my public speaking about recovery. And from what I observed there still, remained a lot of jealousy and envy between Narcotics Anonymous and Alcoholics Anonymous members.

However, I still believed it does not matter whether it's narcotics or alcohol all people in recovery are fighting the battle of addiction and segregating/separating the two was senseless.

If recovery segregation was going to occur it should be for those who only use/abuse narcotics or those who only use/abuse alcohol. But often those who attend N.A. or A.A. are using/abusing both. So, segregating seems senseless to me. It is this belief that has me banned from speaking at; or attending any N.A. or A.A. events or functions.

I knew God was working with me to become a great public speaker when I did a speech on recovery at my community college and one of the judges said I was very loud and almost scared him out of his seat. It was this statement that launched my motivational speaking style and career. During this time, I was completing an Associate of Arts (A.A.) Degree, taking care of kids and working a job that came with a regular paycheck and required me to have a social security card. Life was good, maybe too good. Again, my faith in God and my journey in recovery was going to be tested.

I received a phone call from my sister-in-law that my brother, who was next to me in age had died of an overdose. I instantly felt the pain of losing someone so close to me all over again. My daughters and my son felt the pain as well. They were very, close to their uncle and loved him as much as I did. Losing my brother was very, hard on me and tested my resolve to stay clean (free from drugs). I knew, I still had character defects and was still a work in progress. I fought daily not to pick up the bottle or get high on any drugs. Quite honestly it was difficult because drug use was really the only way I knew to cope. And now I must cope without falling back into my usual routine of self-medication.

My brother saw me start taking my recovery seriously. However, him and my other brothers were still in the street game. My decision to start recovery did not stop my brother who died from an overdose, from having mutual respect for one another. Even when we were physically fighting and arguing with one another, like all siblings do, we knew we loved one another. I really miss my brother a lot. I even dedicated a small book I wrote in recovery to him.

It's all about myself and my brother. I would take the book and a video tape someone made of me public speaking to my college campus. I would put the books and tape in a plastic storage bag and carry them around with me to my college campus, churches, and other places I went and sell them. I would then use the money made from the books sold, to go to the print shop and make more copies of the book. For me it was all about helping others either get into recovery or understand why some people need recovery.

My brother and I had a joke between each other. Every time I started preaching recovery to him. He would say, "Lee, do you hear something?" And I would say, "No, why?" Then he would say, "I do. Gotta Go! Gotta Go!" So, at my brother's funeral I cried and laughed at the same time as I looked down at my brother and said, "Peace be still my brother. Here is my recovery prayer to you. So, now you stay put and hear me out."

It was a struggle, but I stayed sober and continued with my recovery journey, attending college, and speaking to people and different groups about recovery. It was during this time that I remembered an old saying they shared in one of the treatment centers I was in, "The answer to life is learning to live." But to me, I was going to keep on living until I found the answer.

I married again, and my wife was pregnant with my eighth child. We had a beautiful baby girl. The fruit on my tree had grown in the year 2000. I now have seven daughters and one son. I had my private investigators diploma. I graduated from community college and was accepted to a four-year college. And I was raising another child. I also had another marriage that did not last long. And once again my life was going to be tested.

This time it would be with Federal Bureau of Investigations (FBI) Agents. While at work one day I got a phone call from two of my oldest daughters. They said they were at the house with two of my other children and grandchildren. They were being held by the police and my house was being raided! While speeding to get home I received another call on my cell phone telling me to slow down, I 'll get there. I looked in the rearview mirror and saw two police cars behind me. Two police cars on the side of me. And one on each block as we pulled closer to my house.

I was getting upset and angry now. I carried a pistol and had a permit to do so. Why am I being followed? And why are police at my house? The first thing that came to my mind, was what did I do? I had been out of the street game for quite some time and if anything happened to my kids, there was going to be a shootout. Because I will die for mine! As I pulled up to my house that sat on the corner, it was covered by FBI Agents and police. As I approached my home, I was searched by the police outside and then lead into the house.

I saw two of my daughters on the floor in handcuffs and the rest of the kids in the playroom with a policewoman at the door playing guard! The more I saw the more, angry I got! I had not been handcuffed yet, but my children were. And my grandchildren were held in their playroom? Questions were swirling through my head. It was all I could do to stay calm. As questions kept swirling through my head, I was being demanded by the agents to open up my safe. Even as demands were being made I kept asking what is going on?

What did I do? What have I done? Then I heard a familiar sound that I have not heard in years. "JACKPOT!" The FBI Agent said. As I opened my safe and they started pulling out a lot of money, diamond rings. more jewels and a gun; right away I was handcuffed. Then a person from the FBI told me the police had been keeping my house under surveillance. Because it was known that a big drug shipment was coming in and going out this house. Along with many, ladies of the night. Those facts paired with all the things we have from your safe; well, let's just say we know your motive operandi (M.O.).

My anger now changed to a calm and collected attitude. I said, "Sir the women you probably saw, are my biological daughters and their friends that go in and out of this house. And my son and his friends who also come in and out of this house. I am a taxpayer and I have receipts and papers for everything you have taken out of my safe. The bill of sell and insurance for my vehicle, for the firearm, and the badge. I also have a permit for the firearm. Last, but not least can you have one of your police officers run up to McDonald's and get my kids something to eat because its past their suppertime."

One of the police looked at me like I was a smart a** and said, "You just get ready for us to take your black a** downtown. And then we'll have child protection pick up your little kiddie's something to eat." The FBI guy I was talking to looked at me with sort of a smile on his face. He told me to be patient. And shared he was in charge, of this operation. Another FBI agent came in and whispered something in his ear while he was talking to me.

Then one of the police officers went in the living room and took the handcuffs off of my two daughters. Who were then allowed to join my grandchildren that were being guarded by a policewoman in the play-room. Then the handcuffs were removed from my wrists. As the handcuffs were being removed it was shared with me that my family and I were being released but the raid was still under investigation. It was also shared that the FBI would have to hold all the items that were removed from my safe until everything was cleared up. The FBI Agent that was speaking with me also shared he was glad I held my composure around my kids, and just did what I was told.

He then told me, he knows a guy that turned his life around and he is doing very well. He is now too legit to quit! The FBI Agent said to me, "Lee (as he spoke several of my aliases from my past life) You may be a work in progress; but keep doing good! You'll make it. The guy I told you I know who turned his life around is me." Then the FBI Agent walked away. I went back into the house and looked at the mess that needed to be cleaned up while hugging my children.

I immediately started thanking God for sending His angels down to protect us. I felt the police were going to behave differently from what they did because of my criminal background. My older daughters were still upset about the whole ordeal and the traumatic effect that it might have on the little ones. I reminded them of what their great-grandmother would say to me, "If God is for us, then who can be against us?"

My thoughts kept going back to that FBI guy. He too was once a work in progress. I thought now can I be a progress that works? How can I be what a Black man should be about? No more will I let society lock me up and throw away the key. No more will I hide under the blanket of guilt and shame wrapped around the darkness of lies and death. No more will I be a product of hate or representative of failure. I will fight for all people.

I will fight for the young ones who had trouble with the law and cannot find that wall of hope. I will share with them that there is freedom on the other side. I will keep on going to school so I can help them. I will enter the field of criminal justice. I might still be a work in progress but with the support of family and God throwing me a rope of his love and covering me in protection I don't care how many walls are put in front of me. I know the rope that God has given me will not break! Just as long, as I have faith in him.

AN EVERLASTING
TEARDROP

"Let not your hearts be troubled. Believe in God; believe also in me. In my Father's house are many rooms. If it were not so, would I have told you that I go to prepare a place for you? And if I go and prepare a place for you, I will come again and will take you to myself, that where I am you may be also.

—John 14:1-2-3
English Standard Version (ESV)

1 REMEMBER THAT proud moment in 2004 as I walked up to the university stage to receive my Bachelor of Arts Degree in criminal justice law. I finished with a 3.26 grade point average, only points away from the honor roll. My son, my daughters and the rest of the family were very proud of me and my accomplishment. They had a big graduation party for me at Old Country Buffet. It was double joy and happiness for me because my son and his partner had moved their business next door to my business office. So, I got to see him almost every day. We

were already close but seeing each other all the time brought us even closer. My son and I hugged every time we saw each other.

My son married back in 2002. He had four children. And now he was blessing me with another grandchild with my daughter-law Kris. Sometimes they would bring my grandson over to my house for two of my daughters to baby sit. The year 2004 seemed like it was going to be a good year for me. My private investigator and bounty hunting business was doing well. And the security supervisor job I had with the Hope Harbor Building in Downtown Minneapolis was bringing me professional and personal satisfaction. It often made me think I should have tried this living on the right-side thing a long time ago.

Then I got hit with some bad news. One of my homeboys, Paul from back in the day had been killed. He was good for pulling armed robberies and bank jobs (robbing banks). In his life of crime, he had been shot 9 times and still lived. But not this time. He and some other guys pulled a bank job in East Saint Louis, and while Paul was running with a bag of money in his hand, he tried to take some of the money out of the bag. Bad move. The money bag had dye in it, which blew up all over him. Making it easier for the police to spot him. I had a friend named Skip who did the very same thing in a different robbery.

Paul went to prison along with one of my brothers, and when he got out, he started hanging out with my old crew that I pulled armed robberies with. It didn't take long before he was back in the world of crime. I was also told that his ex-girlfriend, who had a restraining order on him caught him coming into her house through a window. She emptied her gun on him. Reloaded and shot him again. I guess she was really scared of him and was making sure he wasn't coming back. People knew Paul was very abusive towards her and many wondered what made her stay with him so long.

I lost a lot of friends from tragic deaths like Paul's. Some of them were lost due to bitter drug wars. Those who did not die on the street are still doing time in prison. The street game is rough. Those who make it out like myself have many battle wounds and tragic street stories. We also owe much to the communities we ravaged. But knowing this still did not prepare me for the news that my son was about to tell me.

That is one phone call I will never forget! I can't remember what time it was. I just remember my phone kept ringing. When I answered, it was my son on the other end of the line. My son was on the other end of the phone crying and saying, "She's Gone Dad! My Wife Is Gone!" I told my son to slow down so I could understand what he was saying. I stayed on the phone a few more minutes to hear what my son was trying to tell me. Once I understood I went to my son.

By the time I got to my son the hurt and pain I heard on the phone was even more evident when I saw him. He lost his best friend, his wife. My daughter-in law was 26 years old. She was a Type I diabetic who died from an insulin reaction. She was found in the bathtub with my three-month old grandson on her shoulder, while Kris (my son's wife) was under water. Her four-year-old daughter found her. She told my son and Kris' dad, that mommy was upstairs in the tub under the water.

My son ran up the stairs behind Kris' dad and found his wife. My son grabbed my grandson before he went under the water. My son was never the same after seeing his wife Kris in the tub with the baby and knowing his daughter had seen it as well. He was in a lot of grief and pain. Because life is often layered and textured my son's wife passing away was not the only matter that made Kris' passing difficult.

Kris' parents were no longer together, and they went through a very, difficult divorce. Kris was her parents only child and Kris' mom was not pleased with her being with my son. Kris' dad let my son, his daughter, and their children live with him. Another situation Kris' mother was not pleased with. I'm not sure why Kris' mother had such strong feelings against my son and her daughter being together. But my observations of her behavior lead me to believe she did not want her daughter to be with, let alone marry a black man.

Kris' dad (a retired police officer) did what he could for his daughter. Unconditional love for sure. Life complications to include Kris being a Type I Diabetic, married with children and a disagreeable mother did not stop him from taking care of his child. I liked Kris' dad because I appreciated the way he loved his child. I had not seen that kind of parental love in my own life, but I was trying to be the kind of parent Kris' dad was to her with my own children.

After my daughter-in-law's death my son and grandchildren continued to live with Kris' father. I tried to be there for my son as much as I could, but he stopped coming to his business. Which meant I was not seeing him weekly. We would talk by phone occasionally and it was during one of these conversations when he told me Kris' mom was trying to get full custody of his children. My son was concerned because he knew Kris' mom did not care for him and was not sure what she would do or say to his children to create a less than favorable opinion of him in their eyes.

After a legal process that seemed to take forever Kris' mom won custody of the children. My son told me a while ago he knew that would happen, because with his police record, he didn't stand a chance in a custody battle. And he knew I could not take full custody of his children because I had my hands was full with the rest of his siblings, my daughters. But my son did get to spent time with his son when his grandmother, Kris' mom was feeling charitable.

My son was going through some pretty, tough times with the passing of his wife. He and his business partner closed-up their office next door to mine. He told me he thought about his wife, the children they had together, and the children he had before he met Kris. It was during this time that he was trying to spend a lot more time with his older daughter and son. It was during this time of thinking and reevaluating that my son shared he would be moving to Duluth Minnesota. He wanted to get away from the city and find some place more peaceful to clear his head. He shared he would stay in touch with me. I told my son, I understood.

We gave each other a hug goodbye. Duluth is about 2.5 hours from Minneapolis. But it made me sad that my son would not be a 5-minute drive away. Although, I did understand why he was leaving the city. My son kept his promise and whenever I needed him or called him, he would come down to the city to see me. I'm not sure if it was the tragic events and life changes happening all around me, but the years seemed to start going by more quickly. 2004 was full of good and bad life changing events, 2005 was a blur and now here it was 2006.

I was working a lot and getting ready to buy a new home. I was legitimate. Something I could never have seen in my younger days. 2005 was a blur as previously stated, but it did include another relationship. For me, love and a happy marriage is the gold standard, so I will try once again. And 2005 was me flying down on another relationship and wanting to get married again.

As my kids are now getting older, they believe they have a say in my relationships. So, if they didn't like who I was dating they had no problem letting the women I was dating know, they came first. And they would say, "If your with our dad we are a family package." In February 2006 I closed on my family's new home in Brooklyn Park, MN. It was a big, beautiful townhouse in a well-kept neighborhood. My son and one of his friends moved everything from our old house to the new house.

I thanked my son for coming all the way down to the city from Duluth to help me. I told him I could only give him and his friend a few dollars. My son started laughing at me and said, "Hey dad you have so many tennis shoes still in the box I just helped myself to a couple pairs so I could break them in for you when I'm playing basketball. The shoes looked real, lonely just sitting up in your closet and stared at me like they wanted me to run somewhere in them." I stared at my son's

6'6" frame as he stood there with this serious look his face and I had a serious look on my face, then we both busted out laughing. I said, "Boy just cause you're 1 inch taller than me don't think I can't still give you a butt whupping." We laughed again and gave each other a big hug while saying, "I love you." As my son drove away with my shoes, I felt he made a good decision moving to Duluth.

As the snow left the ground and the May flowers were springing up all over the place, people were out walking their pets and kids playing in the park. My son came up to my job and brought one of my grandsons to see me. It felt good to see both of them. My son seemed to be slowly rejoining the world. I was telling my son that his sister's birthday was coming up in a few days, June 11th and I would let him know if we were going to do something. I shared I'm not sure right now because I might have to work.

I also shared with my son that I bought another house and would need his help moving some things again. I asked him if he would be available to help me. "Sure dad," he said. "Just let me know. I'll come down to the city and help you." As we gave each other a hug I told him how proud I was of him and to keep depending on God when he needed help. "Love You Dad." Love You Too Son. And my grandson. Have a safe trip home."

A CROSSROAD OF PAIN

Create in me a clean heart, O God, and renew a right spirit within me.

—Psalm 51:10
English Standard Version (ESV)

I KNOW WHAT it is to feel pain. Before reaching my teen years I had already spent years of my life in juvenile and adult correctional, facilities. Before turning my life around. I had to become a father of a murdered child, My Son! My first born was murdered in June 2006. Upon reflecting, I see my life journey has brought me full circle.

I was in my late thirties when my son was getting into trouble. I saw him through me; but could not stop him from going down the wrong path, the same path I did. After a period of time, my son began to turn his own life around. Coming out of street life (the game) my son went into perfume distribution. He was doing very well and was glad to be able to make money without having to worry about the extra layers of shenanigans that came with operating the challenges of street life.

It was June 6, 2006, WAKE UP! This is how fast you are awakened from your peace of mind. Your belief that your children are okay, and all is right in your corner of the world. As I was opening my garage door to go to work two police officers were knocking at my door. They came to tell me my son, my only son, had been murdered. "Not my boy!" I said. But it was my son. The police officers had my son's I.D. I could not hear the voice of the police officers anymore. I felt as though I was in a slow, painful dream that I was not able to awaken from.

When my mind allowed me to return to the present moment, I heard the police officer say, "Someone from homicide will be getting in touch with you soon. Sorry for your loss." The casualness of the delivery from the police officers who told me my only son had been murdered was more than my heart and mind could stand. As the two police officers were walking out the front door, it was as if a strong wind was pushing me to sit down. My brother Melvin was sitting at the kitchen table and heard what had just taken place. He could not speak. Melvin just looked at me in disbelief as the phone rang.

It was a homicide detective on the other end of the line. He called to tell me what happened to my son. The officer told me my son had been shot several times and two young males may have been involved in the shooting. It was information the detective received from my son's girlfriend. She was with my son when he was killed. She told the detective my son had saved her life. The detective told me he wanted to meet with me in person and he did not want me to go to the morgue.

My son no longer physically resembled the young man I knew, and the detective did not want me to see him like that. My mind was bouncing all over the place. I could not believe my son was gone! I think I called my job to share I would not be coming in to work. In this moment things were moving swiftly and in slow motion all at the same time.

I was receiving information from police officers and detectives, processing what I had just been told, and trying to grapple with what my next move should be. That is why I am not sure if I called my job or how my job was informed that I would not be at work that day. I do remember one of the police officers asking me, when was the last time

I had heard from or seen my son. I don't know if I answered the officer. It was as though the whole world stopped.

Mandel, my son came to my job often. He would often bring my grandson and granddaughter with him. My son lived in Duluth, MN but he would come to Minneapolis frequently. My son was dealing with the loss of his wife, Kris who died from an insulin reaction, often caused by the body having too much insulin which causes the blood sugar to drop quickly and drastically. She died at the age of 26. Now, two years later, my son, at the age of 30 was gone. My grandchildren are without their mother and father. I just talked to my son about a week and a half ago. I phoned him and left a couple of messages to tell him I just bought another house and I wanted him to help me move. My son returned my call. He left me a message on my answering machine. The message said, "Dad, this is your son. I got a new cell phone number. Call me." I called my child and called my child and did not get an answer.

As I reflect on this time, I think it's funny how life can take you down memory lane. When going down this lane every minute you had with someone, every moment you shared does not just become important; the moments and memories become magnified because they are all you have of someone who was literally just here. Someone who was literally just a phone call away. Parents often spend their life ensuring their child is well taken care of; planning for them, planning with them, praying them through the difficult times and enjoying as well as appreciating when they made it through the other side of difficult times.

And now in a moment I never saw coming, a moment I never expected; My Son Was Gone! Not my child! Not my son! I won't wake up. I will just keep playing out this dream and when I wake this will be an unpleasant moment that I can dismiss as a bad dream. Suddenly, I heard a voice in my head say Wake Up!! And upon returning to the present moment, I heard the homicide detectives telling me they had some good leads, and they would not rest until my son's killer or killers were behind bars.

In an instant my pain turned to anger. After the police officers left my home, I told my brother, who was just as upset as I was, that I don't want whoever killed my son to get caught. I want them dead. Just like my son. June was one of the coldest and most painful months of my life. Even though the police had kept their promise. They had two young men in custody by the end of June. Both were charged with first degree murder. I was glad they were caught. But them being caught did nothing to relieve my pain.

People think they know how you feel. Unless they have lost a child, they can only guess. The last two hours of my son's life I felt in my spirit he was calling my name. My son knew what kind of work I did (group counseling, certified fugitive enforcement agent). He also knew I carried a badge as well. I always told my son if he got into an argument with someone, walk away. It takes the better person to walk away. I would later find out that my child did what I always told him to do in the situation that led up to his fatal shooting. I will always be proud of my son for doing the right thing. Even as he was doing the right thing it cost him his own life.

The coward that killed my son could not let the argument go. He went and got one of his friends and a .357 gun. The two waited in the backyard, in the dark for my son to come out of the house. My son and his girlfriend were visiting friends. By the time, my son and his girlfriend saw the two men in the backyard it was too late. The men with pistol in hand, open fired on my son. My son pushed his girlfriend back into the house and pulled the door shut. The bullets were ripping through my child's body. The bullets from the gun were emptied into my baby's body.

I call these men cowards because my son was 6'6" and very, strong. If there had been a physical altercation (a fist-to-fist fight), I believe they would have gotten their behinds whupped. I believe a lot of us do wrong in our life, but no one should play God. When people violently take life that is what they do, play god. During the trial, the first-degree murder charge was dropped to second-degree murder. The charge was dropped to second degree murder because my son's girlfriend told the police she was not going to testify if she was not going to be put in protective custody, because she had to live in these streets.

She told my family members she wanted to talk to me and only me about some things. But that meeting never took place because she disappeared and has not been heard from since. I always wonder what my son's last words were, what did they (her and my son) talk about, and how did the argument that lead up to his death start? I remember Mary Johnson and myself sitting in the prosecutor's office. The prosecutor said, "The murderer said if he did not kill my son that night. He was going to kill my child tomorrow."

As I'm listening to the prosecutor tell me what this murderer had said, I'm thinking my whole life is painful at this time. My health, my finances, and my relationships had all taken a turn for the worst. During this time, my support network of my 7 daughters, my pastor, the first lady of my church, the bishop, and my brothers and sisters from the organization, From Death to Life kept me lifted. Without them I don't know what would have happened to me. My pain kept me from checking on my son's brother. This young man was not my biological child, but I gave him my last name. He was an important part of my life and during this painful time I was not there for him. I am ashamed to say that out loud.

Jermaine, my son! I am so sorry I hurt you and through my grief of losing your brother I forgot that you were hurting too. Please forgive me! My 7 daughters; Quina, Kesa, Leelah, Lisa, Carrie, Lesandia, and Kyla all of whom have put their own grief aside to hold their Dad up in hope, prayer, and love. For that I thank you. Many times, I just wanted to keep crying but it has been your love that kept me going. I love each of you with all my heart. Honestly, I felt like God took your brother from us because of my past lifestyle. The naked truth is when I was bad, I was very, good at being bad and thought when I die, I die. Satan had me. I felt I was not worthy of God's grace and mercy.

My son's unnecessary murder reminded me of what my life used to be. It reminded me of not being worthy of God's love. No matter how hard I tried, I was always going to be punished for my crimes. There is a letter that I have been carrying around with me for the past 17 years. When I do speaking-engagements and tell my story, I always read this letter. The letter is called "A letter From Satan." When the devil gets a hold of you, he will not play games with you. He will try to take your will.

As a child I had a learning disability and did not read or write well, which caused me much frustration and failure. My life started with the promise of success and quickly fell into a hole that initially I did not want to be in. But quickly fell into a lifestyle that I not only embraced but thought I enjoyed. This lifestyle I had was filled with many highs, both figuratively and literally; and lows, both figuratively and literally. I had fast money, cars, and women. I even won the Player of the Year Competition which was held in Minneapolis, MN in 1976. As previously shared, I was very, good at being bad.

For those who didn't know what a real player was, I called myself a gentleman of leisure. But in plain English, I was a pimp. And I was very, successful at it. As previously shared in another article I have written "Once Upon A Criminal" I was already in a gang and was a hoodlum by the age of 11. I was smoking cigarettes, drinking, using drugs, and spent time in an adult penitentiary by the time I was 17. To me it was picking up a gun that took me from a hoodlum to a gangster. My pre-teen and young adult years included racking up several felonies to add to my criminal resume'. The time I spent in prison only made me a better criminal not a rehabilitated offender.

I knew who God was through my grandmother's teachings. But I did not have a relationship with God. I do know a lot of people were praying to God on my behalf. I appreciated the prayers. I just had worldly things I thought I needed to make me happy and I was willing to do whatever I needed to do to get them. In looking back, going after worldly goods by any means necessary allowed me to mask the pain I carried. If I look good on the outside and I have everything that others want, I MUST be okay. Not only was I not okay, I was a mess. I did not begin to live until God delivered me.

But now, with my son gone; I died again. I have never dealt with this kind of death. The loss of a child is like no other. As a parent you can prepare yourself for your leaving the planet before your child because that is the natural progression of things. Your hope as a parent is that you are around long enough to spend time with your grandchildren. You feel grateful if your around to see your great-grandchildren. But you can never prepare yourself for the loss of your child no matter how old they are when they pass. Because that is not what is supposed to happen. That is not the natural progression of life's circle.

I remember my daughter telling me I needed to come to church to hear these two mothers speaking and sharing their story about losing a child. They were from an organization called From Death to Life. The organization offers healing groups for parents who have lost children to murder and those parents whose children are serving time in prison for murdering. It was Sunday 2006 when I heard one of the women share about her son who had committed murder and the other mother share her son had been murdered. To see them together was amazing. While listening to these two women speak a spirit came over me that I had never felt before.

I spoke to a gentleman who was affiliated with Parents of Murdered Children, not a name that brings peace or comfort to a grieving parent. I spoke with the gentleman for several hours; but nothing after that. I also tried calling several other organizations in Minnesota and would always get an answering machine. I would leave messages but never received a return phone call. After hearing Mary, one of the women From Death to Life, who spoke at the church; I asked her if I could call her as she was walking out the church door. I told her I needed to talk to a person, not a machine. I told her I was really hurting. Mary told me I could call her anytime day or night.

This is when without even knowing it I was on the road to healing. Mary was so genuine. She even took time off work to give me and my family the support we needed. This is also when I became part of the restorative justice community. And when Tim, Chris, Regina, Mike, Janet, Gwen and Ann became an intricate part of my support network.

From Death to Life had healing groups for women and created healing groups for men. I was a regular participant and facilitator along with Tim but men who have been through this type of life event often keep their feelings locked inside. A few men would attend the healing groups, but not many. I appreciated and still appreciate the opportunity Mary gave me. By Mary offering assistance to men going through what I had experienced promoted healing in me. Mary opening up her organization to me, showed me how unselfish she is. I saw through her actions she is truly a Woman of God.

I remember we used to hold groups at Mary's house. Mary had wicker furniture. Some of the seats looked as though they were about to cave in. I think people attending group would come early to get one of the more, sturdy chairs at Mary's house. I wish my son could have met Mary and got to know her. I know he would have loved her too. I am so glad my son and I had a chance to spend time together but also see the life changes we were both making. My son saw me receive several college degrees, to include a Bachelor of Arts from Concordia University. He saw me work through my private investigator diploma and pursuing a master's degree. He saw me go from being an addict and a drunk to clean recovery and sobriety for many years.

Oh yes, my son saw me change! He also knew the work I had put into changing. Society noticed my change as well. All my felony records were expunged. I had my own bounty hunter business and I was helping law enforcement in many different ways. I also became the director of a women's support group called, Women With Visions of Tomorrow. You may be asking yourself, "Why a women's support group?" My son asked me the very same question. I felt back in the day I had directed women in a negative way, and I can now have a positive impact by directing, affirming, and acknowledging their pain by helping them with their new life purpose.

My son was proud of me! And I was proud of my son too. Especially when he and his business partner surprised me and rented the office space right next door to my office. Our offices were side by side. It was fun to see my son through his office window, working with his clients. He would step out of his office and we would give each other hugs. I know my son was in street life at one time himself. But I was glad and proud to see the change. Even though my son's race may be over I want him to know I am still running the race.

On August 28, 2012 I was diagnosed with cancer. I had to withdraw from my master's program due to being ill from the treatment. But I did not let it stop me from learning. While recovering from cancer I enrolled in an 18-month program on children's literature and received a diploma upon completion. Son, I also became an honorary From Death to Life Board Member, a peace advocate for the northside community, a volunteer facilitator for Victim Offender Dialogue with Restorative Justice, and I facilitate a spiritual recovery group for men and women in distress every week. I am still running the race.

Son I wrote you a letter that I want you to hear. As I stood by that hot summer evening spreading the spirit of you over the Minnesota River, I could not help but ask God if this too is part of the punishment for my crimes. My eyes were filled with tears as I stood there talking to the spirit of my fine young man who once called me Dad. Telling you how sorry I was for not being a better father. And hoping that I could do it all over again. My entire body was numb from the pain that would not stop thumping through my chest.

Oh, how I long to hold you just one more time. And tell you how much I love you. How proud I was that God had chosen me to be your father. Son I am so sorry for the mistakes I made, the lifestyle I chose. I only wish that you did not have to leave us so soon. I want you to know that I love you. And I pray that you are in a better place than this world. I think about you in a song that was written by Harry Chapman *"Cats In the Cradle"* (Chapman, 1976) The lyrics are as follows: *And the cat's in the cradle and the silver spoon Little boy blue and the man in the moon "When you coming home, son?" "I don't know when" But we'll get together then, dad You know we'll have a good time then.*

As children we do not stop to think for one moment to consider how our actions affect the rest of our lives. We live our life day by day according to the hands that life dealt us without being mindful of which kid will be left behind. We only live for the moment and see tomorrow as far away or never coming. As I sit here today telling you my story and looking back on all that I have done in my life I wish I could turn back the hands of time. I wish I could go back to that day I committed my first armed-robbery. I would certainly have stopped myself and the other three boys from robbing that hardware store and leaving with $86.

I wish I would have never celebrated by taking that first drink. It's where my journey into drinking and drug addiction began. Son I'm glad you were able to see me in a different light before you were taken too soon. My life steps are now more intentional and with every accomplishment, every joyous moment, every new memory made I keep you, your brother, your sisters, and Mary at the forefront of my mind. Knowing I am representing God and my family keeps me strong in faith and humble in spirit. Thank You Lord for waking me up this morning.

FRIENDSHIP ROAD

He has delivered us from the domain of darkness and transferred us to the kingdom of his beloved Son, 14 in whom we have redemption, the forgiveness of sins.

—Colossians 1:13–14

AS MARY AND I began attending and speaking at different engagements together our friendship grew stronger. We were asked to speak at Stillwater Prison, Lino Lakes Prison, Moose Lake Prison, Glen Lake Prison, Shakopee Prison, Sauk Center Prison, Rush City Prison, Oak Park Heights Prison, Red Wing Prison, and Saint Cloud Prison. All of which are located in Minnesota and many of which I was jailed at as an inmate.

I can see where the prison has tried to cover up its old façade with new décor. But the new décor sill could not hide the many years of the prison secrets that have killes some, brutalized others, and broken many mentally. These cell blocks are full of pain and the sad part is many in these cells brought the pain with them. They did not need to come to prison to see pain. Seeing several inmates mopping the long hallway floors and hearing thousands of chains rolling as the cell doors closed shut behind us only brought the memories of being an inmate back to me more vividly.

Brought the thought of being a 17 year old in an adult prison. Brought the thought of remembering the doors reminded me of a large mouth monster swallowing me up. And when I was released several years later at 19 years old, the doors still reminding me of a large mouth monster spitting me back out.

It was now August of 2013 and I was struggling a bit with the grief of losing my son. His birthday was coming up in September and he was killed in June. The FDTL Gospel & Jazz on the Lawn was going on. It was an event created for families to enjoy one another and remember their loved ones lost to gun violence. At this event there was a big tree which was used for people to place pictures, drawings, and notes of their loved ones lost to gun violence.

When I was feeling down, I could always go to a true friend who was also my pastor, Pastor Gene. I owe a lot to Pastor Gene. He really is a true man of God. I could see Christ inside him. He clearly understood when life had handed someone a pain that is difficult to bear. His praying and words of encouragement always keep me moving forward. His words provide healing and understanding of forgiveness to my heart. As I was leaving the Gospel & Jazz on the Lawn Event I thought about the friendships I have developed with people who love Jesus and try their best to live by His word, daily.

They were constantly showing me what life with Jesus looks like in action. But why was my heart still questioning, not about God but about myself. Where are the enemies hiding? I know who's putting these negative thoughts in my head. God has shown me through lifelong lessons that He is who He said He is; which is why this questioning is bothering me. I will not let the invisible grief take me back down that pitiful road of anger, hate and revenge. I will stay on the road of friendship, love, and peace. In the name of Jesus we pray, Amen.

WHEN WE DON'T SEE GOD, GOD SEE'S US

"Blessed are those who mourn, for they shall be comforted.

—Matthew 5:4

When a woman is giving birth, she has sorrow because her hour has come, but when she has delivered the baby, she no longer remembers the anguish, for joy that a human being has been born into the world. So also you have sorrow now, but I will see you again, and your hearts will rejoice, and no one will take your joy from you.

—John 16:21–22
English Standard Version (ESV)

SOMETIMES I WONDER when we do bad things and harm to other people do, we really think about the pain we lay on someone else's heart. I know I didn't even think about it when I was out there running the streets. Here it was 2014 and the word murder was still ravaging homes in Minnesota due to prevalent gun violence. Once again, I was not prepared for the tragic event that was about to take place in my life. My oldest daughter's 22-year-old child is the first murder of the New Year. Now my grandson is gone. My daughter's life will NEVER be the same.

And I know she is feeling a pain worse than childbirth!

But this pain will not be going away. This pain will grip her soul infinitely and there is no medicine a doctor can gave you to take the pain away. Losing your child will have you considering using drugs and/or alcohol. Can cause you to become suicidal, when the reality is even if you can find yourself getting a little bit of sleep, you wake up the next day on the cold sidewalk of reality trying to cope. With many understanding what you're going through because they too have lost a child to gun violence; but few willing to talk because of the grief that grips their spirit.

Here I was having been in recovery, taking my own recovery step by step each day; I had the support tools as a recovery counselor to discuss very, difficult topics; I had experienced the death of my own son but had no words for my child who had lost her own child. I had experienced the death of a child (my son) first-hand; I know how the healing and forgiveness process works but I felt helpless. There are no words I could say or anything I could do to ease her pain. I just stood there crying. Holding my child. My child who had just lost her child to murder.

I was just praying that even though she isn't seeing/feeling God right now, that God is seeing her. Seeing her pain! And I know He is not going to leave my child in this suffering and turmoil. I know God will hold on to her hand as she walks down the road of healing. Just like He continues to hold on to my hand. My daughter and I will see God and the sons each of us have lost to gun violence in heaven one day.

2015 was very, busy for me. I was doing a lot of recovery speaking to/with groups and on a few cable tv and news programs about my son's murder, my past activity as an offender; and turning my life around with the help of God. I was still involved with the Minneapolis Juvenile

Center Gun Program. I was also invited to a love and forgiveness conference in Amman, Jordan in the country of Israel. There was already a
lot going on in Syria and the terrorist group ISIS was on the rise. Mary
my friend from Death to Life was now my wife. And we along with
four other Americans from their organizations that dealt with gun
violence, restorative justice, and forgiveness; were invited to a conference arranged by the Salam Institute for Peace and Justice, which was
based in Washington DC. So, in collaboration with the Royal Institute
in Amman Jordan, the conference would be held in Israel with the USA
funding the four-day trip.

The purpose of the conference was to share our stories about
forgiveness and healing. To provide a positive example of love which
could possibly help to build a positive platform of peace and love
between different societies. I have been to Mexico and Jamaica and saw
how the rich and poor lived. But to be able to walk on the same ground
that Jesus walked; was a humbling experience. The American group of
six people also felt a part of history because, of what had taken place
in Amman, Jordan February 2015.

Tragedy struck Jordan and the King of Jordan had to fly back
from the USA (as he was meeting with President Obama) to Jordan in
a hurry.

Published by the Jordan Press Foundation   www.jordantimes.com

THE JORDAN

Rest in Peace Muath

Wednesday, February 4, 2015 | Rabi II 14,1436 Hijri

Jordan vows 'earth-shaking' respon

King cuts short US visit, urges Jordanians to unify in face of tragedy

By Khetam Malkawi

AMMAN — Jordan on Tuesday threatened an "earth-shaking response" for the burning alive of Jordanian pilot Muath Kasasbeh by the so-called Islamic State (IS) terrorist group, while His Majesty King Abdullah urged Jordanians to stand united at these crucial times.

Following the release of a video showing a group of IS masked terrorists burning Kasasbeh alive, the Jordan Armed Forces-Arab Army (JAF) issued a statement saying that the officer was killed on January 3, nine days after his F-16 crashed over Raqqa in northeast Syria *(see text of the army statement in separate story).*

In his statement, aired on Jordan TV, King Abdullah described IS as a cowardly terrorist group that has nothing to do with true Islam, praising Kasasbeh as a brave pilot who was

Photo by Osa...

Jordanians rally near the Interior Ministry Circle in Amman on Tuesday following the news of Muath Kasasbeh's exe... the terror group Daesh

dullah would cut short his visit to the US, with the White House announcing an unscheduled meeting between the King and Presi...

army vowed a response that is "proportionate to the magnitude of the tragedy of all Jordanians", according to the statement read on Jor...

ment Spokesperson Mohammad Momani, who said several measures will be taken by the Kingdom to respond to this brutal group.

Jordanians' will devastate ranks".

Addressing who had doub... the brutality o...

Back in the states, the months seem to move by quickly. It was already 2016. I was working, volunteering, and speaking. I had two bouts with cancer and throat surgery. But thank God in the name of Jesus I was still going strong. I've traveled to Washington D.C., Georgia, Wisconsin, Atlantic City, New Jersey, and New York speaking on forgiveness and recovery. The dream of opening up a school for victims and offenders living under one roof in the name of peace was still in me. For years I've had this vision. And I knew it could work. But no one wanted to fund the idea.

I didn't understand why. I thought it was because I wanted to work with both victims and offenders? I knew getting closer to God made me see this is my purpose. Later that year I became a licensed ordained minister. I was already facilitating spiritual recovery group meetings. People would flock to the community room when I was speaking at my church. In my own private prayer time I would often share with the LORD I CAN'T SEE YOU BUT YOU CAN SEE ME, HEAR MY PRAYER AND SEE MY VISION.

It was the spring of 2017; and it happened! I was talking to an old friend of mine who was in the property business. In the past, some of my bounty hunter agents and myself had done security work for him. He heard my idea for victims and offenders recovering from drug abuse together and helping them overcome the societal barriers that often held them back or returned them to drug abuse and criminal activity while providing them with a mindset of redemption. And he partnered with me right away. I thought about what my recovery mentor used to say, "Dang what people say! Watch what they do."

I wrote a play that would be the kick-off to my victim and offender redemptive program. To provide people and potential funders with a vision of what the program would be.

Victims & Offenders Recovery Community
College (V.O.R.C.) computer lab

The play was held in north Minneapolis on West Broadway at the Capri Theater. Where Prince, The Time and other musical artists from the Twin Cities got their start. The play I wrote was a musical called, "It's Me." It's about true things that were going on in the community of north Minneapolis and surrounding areas: bullying, sex trafficking, murder, fallen police officers, drug abuse, racial profiling, and suicide.

It was hard to find actors and performers in the arts community to play the parts that brought the play to life. But with the help of my church; Joint Heirs With Christ Faith International and my teenage daughter, grand-daughter, Victims & Offenders Recovery Community College (V.O.R.C) agreeing to help and play the parts in the play; my idea was no longer a blueprint., now it a house! With six V.O.R.C members (three who had been victims of crime, and three who had committed crimes) now sitting at the V.O.R.C School House dining room table, breaking bread together and discussing the play. What a sight for me, to see this happening.

Reverend Roy's Play "It's Me"

Cast of "It's Me"

As time went on, by Jan of 2018 with just a handful of volunteer staff, the V.O.R.C. started managing a 4.5 million dollar apartment complex that now housed the V.O.R.C. The forty-seven unit building was made available for men and women on both sides of criminal matters and recovery (alcohol and drug abuse). This non-profit recovery college is very, successful to this day. And the people I have partnered with have been very committed to this type of programming. One man even went into his own savings to keep V.O.R.C afloat.

In May of 2019, my sister died. This was a very, bad blow to me. It was sad how she died. But out of respect and love for my sister I will not share that at this time. I took my sister's death hard and was not able to take time off from work to grieve. I loved my job with the Salvation Army and the people I met that used the services and the people who worked there. But after 22 years of working a legit job (that still makes me smile) and 23 years of being sober (that makes me smile even harder), it was time for me to retire from my job and focus more on the V.O.R.C. Program I created.

I left my job in September of 2019. November 5, 2019, I had a heart attack. And had to have triple bypass heart surgery. How's that for a life full of very high, highs and interesting lows. But wait! The story doesn't end here, stay tuned for the final chapter.

THE FIELD OF HEALING: REFLECTIONS BY REV. ROY

Eager to maintain the unity of the Spirit in the bond of peace. There is one body and one Spirit—just as you were called to the one hope that belongs to your call.

—Ephesians 4:3–4

A new commandment I give to you, that you love one another: just as I have loved you, you also are to love one another.

—John 13:34
English Standard Version

HERE IT IS January of 2020 and wouldn't you know it the world has not stopped spinning out of control. With a worldwide pandemic, the death of George Floyd that brought police brutality to the forefront for many and a continuous reminder for others, racism, riots and chaos covered with coats of political destruction and mayhem. It makes you wonder if the world was ever meant to be a harmonious place.

The turmoil reminds me of a story when two strangers met in an open paperless field. These two strangers could only see each other's hearts through pen and paper. As they were both blinded by the pain they were born into which led them to this field of unspoken words. For they could not see each other's faces. One stranger's life was filled with pain locked up inside him. The grief he held so close was caused by the pain only a parent, a father knows when their child has been murdered; by young men who were Black like his son.

The second set of strangers are two young men who caused this pain. Pain the first stranger held close because he could not understand why these strangers would put him through such an ordeal. One of the young men (whom I will only call stranger because it hurts too much too speak his name), stood by and watched his partner gun down my son. My son who was a father himself. Both strangers are now doing countless years in prison. One, for just being there watching. And the other for doing the actual shooting. One of the strangers reached out to the father who lost their son. The other stranger never reached out.

The stranger whose title is father and the stranger whose title is criminal agreed to meet in a paperless field for one to ask for redemption and for the other to decide if he is able to accept it. While an angel in heaven stands by watching. Let the journey of the two strangers in a paperless field begin.

Stranger I:
Father to father, look what's been done, you stood by while they murdered my son, he wasn't just a father, he was my child, now I cover my face with silence tears and a shameful smile.

God you said you would not put on me no more than I could bare, but with all this senseless killing Lord, does anybody care.

My son was so vibrant, so full of life,he was my child and he hated strife, my son meant the world to me, this Stranger must know, it was not easy, letting him go.

Or family lives so drastically changed, what was the purpose of this foolish exchange?

Stranger 2:
I am writing you to Apologize for what I had done, for my participation in giving the other person the gun that killed your son.

I am so terribly sorry for the pain I cost your family, and for what I did, my loyalty went to friends, please believe me, I was just an immature kid. After learning and serving all this prison time, I want to be able to help other young ones. In the community not to commit crimes.

The police doctors and politicians care about him as being a man then we can all stop a bullet with our hands.

Stranger 1:
I received your letter Stranger,
I read it over and over till I felt a certain way.
There are questions about my son's death that need answering, to this very day.

Your letter stuck in my mind, while I've been on this Spiritual course, and within my heart, I felt your remorse.

I'm glad to hear that you are doing ok and you're taking a stand. To right the wrongs in your life and to become a better man.

I had forgiven you sometime ago, even with my heart and body still aching in woe.

My family may not understand or may even disagree, but in Gods eyes I was blind; but now I can see.

It is not for me to judge you or for me to hate, vengeance is mine sayeth the Lord our souls to take.

I hope to hear from you soon Stranger, until then stay safe and well. And remember to keep away from Satan's tall lies and his sneaky tales.

Stranger 2:
I got your letter, and I want to thank you for reaching out to me. It was beyond anything I would've never expected or even believed.

When I heard from you, I had prepared myself to read your words of anger and hate. Not to read your words of love, mercy and grace. It took me to another place in my heart that I was feeling, a place that was leaving me with some kind of peace and healing.

For so many years let it be told, I wanted to tell you how sorry I was for being so cold, the negative lifestyle that some of us kids grow into, will have you do things you can't undo. For all the years I am locked up, and for all the years to come. No time can replace your family loss, no time can give you back your Son.

I want you to know Stranger, that I hear you and your family weep and cry inside these walls, and any question's you want to ask me I will in all honesty answer them all.
So in part Stranger, I will leave the rest up to you.
Sincerely: Stranger 2.

Stranger:1

It was good to hear from you Stranger, and your safe and in good health, and that you knew and understood how me and my family felt.

On my son's birthday I dreamed about you as well as him, and wondered if the two of you would of loved each other like black brothers, or would the chances have been very slim.

When my son was a baby, I use to play with him and sing him songs. My main questions to you is, why was my son murdered? What did he do so wrong?

The grief in my heart is already painful and sad, but what makes the pain more excruciating is explaining to my grandchildren, why they don't have a dad.

Even with our shameful moments in writing each other in this land of uncertainty, God put us in this paperless field for a reason, which only he can see

What happened that dreadful night, did my son get into an argument or a fight?
Though my life healing and forgiveness has started me anew
I wish for that same kind of peace, love, and forgiveness for you.

Stranger:2

I received your words and they touched my heart, which compels me to tell you more of my story that may pull our friendship apart.
I had not been completely honest with you and it hurts me to say, that only God knew that I wanted to tell you what happened in every way.

Your son didn't do anything wrong you see
There was no fight, no argument,
I didn't know him, and he didn't know me,
It was on all based on a lie that one of my friends had said.
And the rest of the untruths just went to my head.

I am so sorry for the words I kept from you, as I saw your son's shadow
standing on the darkened doorstep. When my friend hollered out your
son's name, the late-night air was lit up with bullets of shame. After
that we ran away trying to hide, not knowing that your son had died

it was more than serving prison time here that was eating me up inside,
it was me telling you the truth! and telling you why? As I stood by and
watched your son being murdered, I was bound by pain and did not
see I do know the one who pulled the trigger and shot your son dead,
was me!

Stranger: I
How dare you! When I first received your words, I thought to myself;
all the repeat hate, anger and pain; again boiled up inside of me, you
can't even imagine how I felt, but here's the part I didn't understand
the part I could not see; why did I hate that kid, but still care about the
man! I guess what I am trying to say is, through my son, bringing God's
love and peace to everyone.

We were brought together in this paperless field for a reason!
The lord knows what He's doing in every season.
He knows of the spirit that is in our hearts, even though, we are miles
apart. Maybe our loved ones in the upper room aka heaven also know
what we both are feeling, that's why our words are written in this
paperless field of the healing.

Stranger:2

There really isn't much I can say to express how humbled and aston-
ished I am by your grace. I pray our loved ones, lost are in a better
place. While thinking about your son, I just want to share these last
words with you, and hope you understand, the title is: I Can Stop a
Bullet With My Hands.

I can stop a bullet with my hands...
Just let me hug the child,
let me push him in a swing
while he screams with joy,
and rides the waves of his laughter
unhampered by dread.

I can stop a bullet with my hands...
Just let me take him out for ice cream
and then bring him to a museum where
he can see his power through his ancestors'
achievements let me teach him about himself
and his endless possibilities.

I can stop a bullet with my hands...
Just let me feed that little boy
with nourishing food,
let me be there for him after school
and help him with his homework.
Let me take him on trips
beyond his neighborhood.

I can stop a bullet with my hands...
Just let me raise his conscious
as I respect his mother,

and move with kindness and compassion
through our streets.
Let me support his dreams
while he's awake
and keep him safe and warm
while he's asleep.

I can stop a bullet with my hands...
If you just help me!
Show that little boy he's valuable,
let him see that his teachers,
the police, doctors, and politicians
Then we can stop a bullet with our hands too.

REFERENCES

Curry, A. (2010, July). Black Stone Rangers/Black P. Stone Nation/El Rukns. Retrieved from https://www.blackpast.org/african-american-history/blackstone-rangers-black-p-stone-nation-el-rukns-c-1957-c-2000/

Chapin, H., Chapin, S. (1974). Cats in the cradle [Recorded by Harry Chapin].
On Verities & Balderdash Elektra Records.

English Standard Version Study Bible (ESV). (year). Publisher. (Original work published).
Hennepin Avenue pictures (n.d.)
https://www.bing.com/videos/search?q=pictures+of+1960%27s+hennepin+avenue+minneapolis&qpvt=pictures+of+1960%27s+hennepin+avenue+minneapolis&FORM=VDRE

Henry's Hamburgers (n.d.) Retrieved from https://www.bing.com/images/search?view=detailV2&ccid=Xld8W87g&id=C8B07F8C2FB70098AF814457548F896A109CFF-8B&thid=OIP.Xld8W87gMvU3EOXGsBaDzwHaIg&me-

diaurl=https%3A%2F%2Fs-media-cache-ak0.pinimg.
com%2F564x%2Fed%2F86%2F75%2Fed86759cd3a03afe0d-
33353bcff4852b.jpg&exph=640&expw=557&q=old+hen-
ry%27s+hamburger+minneapolis&simid=6079937157
45751630&ck=09717861B433855326FD91A880AE0AD-
F&selectedindex=4&qpvt=old+henry%27s+hamburger+minne-
apolis&form=IRPRST&ajaxhist=0&vt=0&sim=11

Malkawi, K. (2015, February 4). Jordan Earth-Shaking Response. *The Jordan*

MNOPEDIA (n.d.). 1967 Plymouth avenue riots. Retrieved from
www.mnopedia.org/event/civil-unrest-plymouth-avenue-min-
neapolis-1967

Nacirema Minneapolis (n.d.) Retrieved from
https://www.bing.com/images/search?view=detailV2&c-
cid=cDsJ9yLW&id=433D0406E195B39A2A1F48B4E70D-
B46C005FC3E8&thid=OIP.cDsJ9yLWOE00cvybGx-
1u7AAAAA&mediaurl=https%3a%2f%2fth.bing.
com%2fth%2fid%2fR703b09f722d6384a2872fc9b1b1d6eec%3fri
k%3d6MNfAGyoDeeoSA%26riu%3dhttp%253a%252f%2
52ftwincitiesmusichighlights.net%252fwp-content%252fup-
loads%252f2015%252f05%252fnaciremaclub1975.jpg%26e-
hk%3dkHs8iByhs%252f28DI7qu2ZqYm7xnBesgl%252fp-
CU%252bACvzzJLw%253d%26risl%3d%26pid%3dImgRaw&-
exph=216&expw=361&q=pics+of+nacirema%2c+minneap-
olis&simid=607990056403996522&ck=C93B4C3A37A4F-
3C73B7747F8B727A622&selectedIndex=0&qpvt=pics+o
f+nacirema%2c+minneapolis&FORM=IRPRST&ajaxhist=0

The Prison Mirror. (2008, February 20). Vol. 121

Red Wing Correctional Facility Retrieved from
https://www.bing.com/images/search?view=detailV2&c-cid=tKI4Dhou&id=928BF30599EC343289E01A20C-80C90D71DE54A0A&thid=OIP.tKI4DhouGRHc7ttoqkip-RAAAAA&mediaurl=https%3A%2F%2Falchetron.com%2Fcdn%2Fminnesota-correctional-facility--red-wing-e50dee80-d3f9-4e15-8810-ef339f96776-resize-750.gif&exph=349&expw=468&q=red+wing+correctional+facility+pics&simid=608013305122457420&ck=198E49D75DAC409D50E3F-1520BA54348&selectedindex=11&qpvt=red+wing+correction-al+facility+pics&form=IRPRST&ajaxhist=0&vt=0&sim=11

Simon, A., Ransohoff, M. (Executive Producers). (1965–1971). *The beverly hillbillies* [TV Series]
Filmways Productions; CBS Television Network, CBS Television Distribution

Stewart, R (1971). Maggie may On *Every Picture Tells A Story* [Album]. Mercury.

Taschner, T. (1993, May 3). Former Gang Member Helping Clean Up A Suburban 'Hood'.
Star Tribune

Thomas, G. (2007, November 27). Beyond today: Can you break the cycle of generational dysfunction. Retrieved from
https://www.ucg.org/the-good-news/can-you-break-the-cycle-of-generational-dysfunction

Wikipedia (n.d.). Black power fist. Retrieved from https://en.wikipedia.org/wiki/Black_Power

The Prison Mirror

Prison Magazine

FAMILY PHOTOGRAPHS

Rev. Roy's sister

Rev. Roy's grandmother

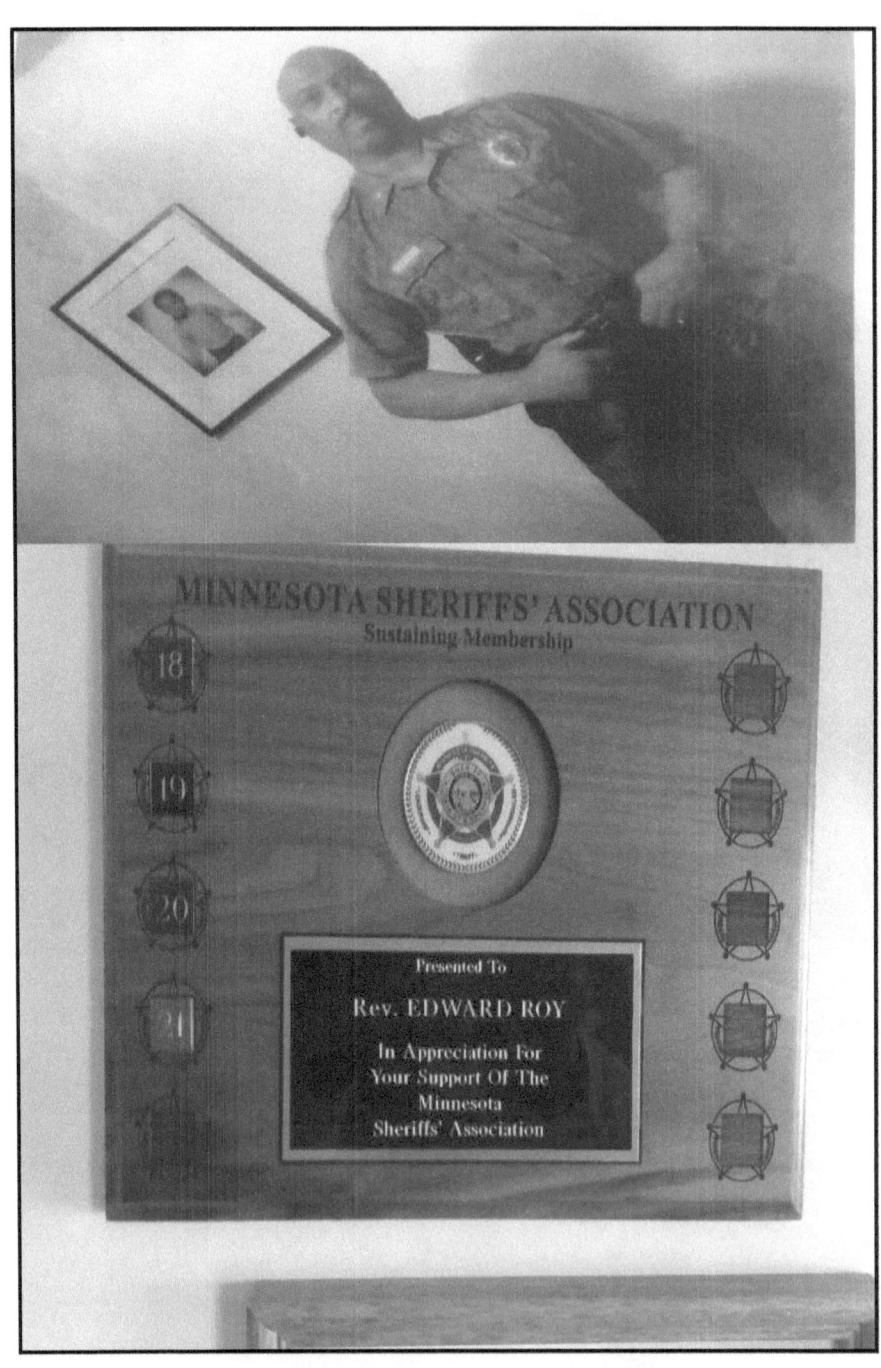

Rev. Roy